MISS ADVENTURES

BY LISA GREYHILL

D1059865

Cornerstone Press
2006

First 2006 Printing

Printing, collating, and binding by:
Worzalla Publishing
3535 Jefferson St.
Stevens Point, WI 54481-0307

Printing made possible by the generous
contributions of Worzalla Publishing.

This book was printed in the United States.
Library of Congress Cataloguing Number: 2006936965
ISBN 0977480240

Cover design by Colin McGinnis
Photos © Lisa Greyhill, Ren Herr, and Guy Johnson

Contact information:
Dan Dieterich, Professor of English
Tutoring and Learning Center, LRC
University of Wisconsin-Stevens Point
Stevens Point, WI 54481-3897
(715) 346-2849
dan.dieterich@uwsp.edu

Cornerstone Press
University of Wisconsin – Stevens Point
Stevens Point, WI

This book is for Kevin, Mom and Dad.

Table Of Contents

I.   Acknowledgements

VII.   Introduction

3.   Horse Leg

19.   Home, Home on the Mongolian Range

33.   A Summit Celebration of Sorts

45.   The Truth About Lenticular Clouds

69.   Meeting the Mountain Moai

87.   Alien Plateau

105.   I Am Survived

Julie —
Keep the adventure alive
my friend !
WW

Travel is fatal to prejudice, bigotry, and narrowmindedness.

Mark Twain

LISA GREYHILL

ACKNOWLEDGEMENTS

This book is the result of a 20-year relationship that has simmered quietly in the back of my mind since my days in Professor Dan Dieterich's *Editing and Publishing* class. In his class I self-published *The Complete College Party Guide* and *Real Trivia* – both projects I enjoyed immensely.

Professor Dieterich's class taught me a great deal about what it takes to be an editor and publisher, but it was the proverbial "tip of the iceberg." Compared to the organization that now exists as Cornerstone Press, one would think I'd chipped *Real Trivia* on stone tablets. What was once a project for a team of one today requires the coordinated effort of a whole staff – and the difference is significant. I feel like the grandmother that leans over and pinches your cheek with a "my, how you've grown!"

I thank all those at Cornerstone Press who have had my manuscript pass through their hands. They have shown my work great respect and it has benefited from their creativity, thoroughness, and energy: Dale Bratz, Jr., Nelson Carvajal, Felicia Ciula, Donna Collins, Tara Cook, Peggy Farrell, Amanda Fisher, Aimee Freston, Maggie Hanson, Daniel Henke, Andrew Ilk, Sara Jensen,

Colin McGinnis, Christine Mosnik, Ingrid Nordstrom, Trina Olson, Ryan Ostopowicz, Michael Philleo, Joy Ratchman, Jason Roskos, David Stetler, Andrea Vesely, Chris Warren, Jennifer White, and Chuck Zoromski.

A sincere thank you to Dan Dieterich for his encouragement and good counsel of twenty years ago. Merci! also to Diane Dieterich for her generous hospitality and to their dogs Yukon and Sarge for all the happy licks.

My girlfriends, especially Kathy Olson (KO), Alison Graeme, Jennifer Coghlan, Gerianne Billo, Roxana Vergara, Jill Jacobs, and Linda Fournier read drafts, dug through photos, drank many bottles of wine, and/or were with me on at least one adventure even if it wasn't mentioned here – you guys are the BEST friends!

If I could create a new rose for her garden I would give it to Marti Dee, who has been Mom2 to me since my days of skinned knees and a sunburned freckled nose. In the dark winter months Mom2 shared her own prose and critiqued my stories via email keeping me on track while also allowing me to read her lyrical writing.

To the talented Lew Freedman, Arnie Bernstein, Barry Keefe and Larry Gerber whom all have provided me great support from their own special corners of the media world, muchas gracias!

I raise my Nalgene bottle to all the fantastic local outfitters around the globe whom I love and who care for my clients like family: Ed Deacy my fearless and good humored leader in the Boundary Waters; Kennedy, Bongo, and Willy in Tanzania; Annie and Rose in Kenya; Stefanie, Sijani and Mandingo on Zanzibar; Pepe in Peru; Hishey in Bhutan; Te, Lan and Golp in Thailand; Diane and Ray in the Mediterranean; all their staffs, and so many others. Stateside, Diana Kollaritsch, Donna Montana, Diane Walz, John Panella and Nancy Leckie at The Travel Team generously shared their knowledge and support through the years and took care of my travelers whenever I was out of the country. I couldn't have done it without you!

Saving the best for last, I know where all this really started – at home. To my parents, John and Dorothy Gay, who gave love freely and dealt discipline with a hug of thanks each time my siblings and I survived the adventures of our youth. To Maura, Brian, Paul, Sean, Michelle, and Geoff and their spouses and children with whom I've had more adventures than could ever be told – especially as it would probably give Mom and Dad simultaneous heart attacks. To Grandpa Gay and Grandma Delaney, whose spirit and love of life I carry with me every day. To merely say "Thank you" doesn't begin to convey what's in my heart for each of you.

And especially I thank Kevin with whom I now share all my adventures. There are no more powerful words than "I believe in you."

To all those whom I've failed to mention by name but who have been a part of my life and the Adventure Travelers Society for the past ten years: Asante Sana!

THE ADVENTURE GOES ON!

LISA GREYHILL

INTRODUCTION

When my friend Kathy (best known as KO) suggested that I start an adventure travel business back in the 90's it sounded like a fun idea for a business. Little did I realize the impact that the *Adventure Travelers Society*, as it became known, would have on my life and on the lives of many of the people with whom we have come in contact.

We created ATS to provide global adventures as well as a means for like-minded travelers to meet. Soon social clubs of our travelers sprung up in Illinois and Wisconsin, and members from all over the US began maintaining friendships and traveling together again and again.

Despite the myriad challenges, I discovered that what I was doing was not just making a living but changing people's lives. Joe and Julie, now parents of two beautiful girls, met on one of our trips to the Peruvian Amazon. Katie joined us at the end of a difficult divorce—the start of a healing process that brought her to a new relationship and group of friends. We helped our outfitters in Tanzania to start their own business, which has in turn provided jobs to many men and women from their village on the side of Kilimanjaro and contributed to the improvement of their school. Our members generously donated money to help our friends in Thailand recover after the tsunami, and they also donated their time to such efforts as the

River Rescue and to teaching children in remote areas of Tibet, Peru, and Africa. And there are dozens of similar stories.

But I had a greedier personal reason for staying the course: all these adventures were supplying me with fodder for some pretty funny stories. Sure, in this book I could easily poke fun at the individuals who were themselves odd, arrogant, ridiculous, or otherwise "N-1" where "N" equals the total number of people on a trip, and "minus 1" equals that one individual who just isn't going to fit in…. but I've decided instead to take the path of least resistance and tell a few tales of what has happened to me on some of my travels.

A few of these stories happened when I was with clients, but just as many came from trips when I was on my own or with friends.

Some people selling "adventure" might consider the stories in this book to be business suicide. Let them sit smugly in judgment as they pack off another ski group to the Rockies or run a "golf adventure" to Vegas. Most of those people consider a three-star hotel in an urban area to be an adventure.

Anyone in the industry worth their salt knows that sometimes things just go wrong, and the results (given enough time, distance, a hot shower, and a decent meal) can be pretty funny.

HORSE LEG

Costa Rica is a lush and mountainous country located between Nicaragua and Panama, warmed to the east by the Caribbean and cooled by the waters of the Pacific Ocean on the west. I had combined a private property inspection with a larger meeting so that I could get the most of my time and invited my friend Jack to join me, as I knew his adventurous spirit would stand up fine on this rather seat-of-the-pants trip.

Bobby, a fellow member of a private club in Chicago, owned the private property I was to inspect. Wealthy, good-looking, and fun, Bobby would be considered a great catch for any girl except for his addiction to drugs and alcohol. I had never known anyone with an addiction like his. Though now clean (again), courtesy of the Betty

Ford Clinic, I could sense that the desire to use itched constantly just below the surface.

Bobby had been down at his house in the mountains of the west coast for a week, and he was pleased to announce upon our arrival that in addition to owning his mountain property, he was about to close on a beachfront house as well. Shall we celebrate with a beverage?

We found ourselves in this spirit a few days later on our way down from the mountain house to the beach property to celebrate Bobby's birthday and his first night of official ownership. A local friend of his, a drunken French resort property owner named Michel, was planning a surprise party at his beach bar about three homes away from Bobby's new house. That meant a night of as much drinking as everyone could stand in a community full of professional drunks.

"One best be prepared to wear their big boy pants in this crowd," I thought as I threw some things into my backpack for the night. I'm no prohibition crusader, but Bobby's addiction was so strong that he would wake at 5:00 each morning and roust the rest of us for a drive to a little roadside place for his first beer of the day. In Bobby's world, beers were like water and primarily used for hydration. And they went really well with Jose's scrambled eggs.

So we bounced down the dirt mountain

road in ATVs because no other vehicle could make it up or down the steep, unpaved grade, heading for Bobby's beach house and his surprise birthday party as my pack of essentials thumped me in the back with every bump. The sun had set and we headed straight for Michel's—it was time to *seriously* start partying. My pack sat at my feet while I sipped on a beer and watched the same people get tanked that got tanked the night before and the night before that. I never even bothered to reach into my pack for my jewelry (who would notice?) or to pull out my camera to capture the "surprise" moment when the birthday boy walked through the door.

The party was made up of mostly "local" people—that is to say, foreigners rich enough to buy property in Costa Rica, a smattering of paying resort guests, Jack, and me.

I spent some time talking to Dieter, a German who had a work schedule that allowed him to live in Costa Rica for several months at a stretch. A true German, I thought. Dieter had built his house by hand, an open-air fort of one small square "bedroom" surrounded by a large deck which housed his kitchen consisting of a coffee pot and hot plate surrounded by railings to hang all the things that inevitably got wet in the regular rains. Here Dieter could live the simple life with minimal electricity and running water and focus his energies on his true love—soccer. Dieter was apparently a great soccer player and all the different local teams sought him out. Dieter's soccer skills and his fluent Spanish had allowed him to get to know many of the local people.

Behind the bar Michel was popular because he was the owner and drunk much of every day. While he wanted his beach rental units and bar to make money, it didn't seem too important how much he actually took in each night. He poured drinks freely and charged for about every third one. At Michel's place you'd find the other foreign alcoholics. It provided a safe haven for displaced people in denial. Thus, the party was a big success.

Jack and I, unaccustomed to such devoted drinking from sunrise to sunset, were pretty much "*beered* out" early on and left the party hoping to do some body surfing. We walked along the shore to Bobby's new beach house. I dropped the pack on his patio picnic table before we waded out into the water. Standing knee-deep in light rollers, we watched a storm come in. Flashes of lightening lit up the beach imprinting images of houses and people on the waterfront temporarily burned into our retinas. The previous night we had body surfed ourselves into exhaustion. The phosphorus plankton lit up breaker after breaker decorating us with twinkling constellations of light as we tumbled through the water. But tonight was a bust. The Pacific was once again dark and quiet, so we headed back to the beach house letting ourselves in through the front door.

"Did you grab the pack?" I asked Jack.

"No, I thought you got it," he said. We both made for the door that opened onto the beach patio, threw it open, and stared at an empty table. I suddenly recalled the image of a person on the beach by our house. At the time I thought it was the fourth person in our party, an obsequious friend of Bobby's nicknamed Cash, who was clearly desperate to get laid. I was a little surprised that he had left the party early figuring that he'd surely find some drunken woman to help him out. Now back at the house, I realized that I had assumed wrong... he wasn't here, nor was my pack.

"Oh shit," we said simultaneously and yanked the door shut as we started running down the beach back to the party. "They've got my passport!" I cried. "I'm leaving for Mongolia and China in two weeks and I *need* that thing!"

"My new digital camera was in there!" Jack said.

"Oh no!" I wailed, "My camera *and* jewelry were in there too!"

Breathless we barged in on the festivities and blurted out, "We've been robbed!" "They have my passport!" I wailed. With hardly two words,

Dieter ran out, jumped on his motorcycle and rode off into the night.

"What was that all about?" I asked. Michel explained that Dieter played for several local soccer teams and probably had good connections with the thieving community. With any luck, he would find my backpack or at least my passport.

He offered me a free shot. Jack got one too though his losses were considerably less. The remainder of the partiers joined in, hating to miss out on free booze. They raised their glasses in a sympathetic toast. "Bummer!" they cheered and tossed back their shots before returning directly to their conversations.

Thank you for the deep sentiment of sympathy.

We returned stunned and depressed to Bobby's and called it a night, a haze of tequila lingering in my palette of teeth that would not get brushed. We headed off to our rooms to sleep in the clothes we'd worn all day as our belongings were now in someone else's possession. I didn't even want to think about my camera and jewelry. And then it started to rain.

Bobby awoke for his 5 a.m. beer and rousted us all out of bed. I wanted to keep sleeping, to not think about having to replace my passport at the US consulate in San Jose so that I could get out of Costa Rica and back home where I'd have to put in a rush order for visas for China and Mongolia *again*, before my departure. What a mess. Even the weather was crummy.

Bobby decided the best way to put this behind us was to go back to the mountain house where we had more clothes. Besides, if it was going to rain we may as well not waste our time on the beach. We piled onto the ATVs and buzzed our way through the little coastal village and back up the side of the mountain.

At the mountain house, diversions were few as there was no television and reading options were scarce. Ever restless, Bobby initiated water sports in the river that ran near his house. Bobby's property consisted of half the mountain, vertically split, that included a small farm toward the base of the mountain and about a dozen good-size waterfalls and a river that started high above his house. Last night's rain had the river running full and the waterfalls spilled over into deep pools beneath each fall where we played rag tag, flinging ourselves off the rocky tops and plunging into the cool water below to avoid getting smacked with a wound up wet towel.

When we tired of chasing each other around, we grabbed the inflatable rafts and tubes and bobbed in the rapids, wedged between rocks, until we were all wrinkled. All the running, slipping and jumping had me happily forget my concerns, but once I was reclining on the raft I began again to worry of my stolen passport. I wondered if Dieter would have any success. I had already negotiated with the devil: "they can keep everything else, just get my passport back," was the last thing I had said to Dieter as he rode off into the night.

Restless again, Bobby was on the move. "Come on!" he said. Back at the house, Bobby called for his horses, hopeful that a ride to the top of the mountain would help me forget my troubles for another hour or two. "Thank you, Bobby. I'd love to," I smiled. No sense in raining on everyone else's parade. After all, I had allowed my pack to be stolen by trustingly leaving it unattended—even if we were conscientious enough to put it in sight on a table against a house on private property on what appeared to be a rather deserted beach.

Bobby's mountain rose several hundred feet above the house, and I decided I'd enjoy spending an hour or so ascending on horseback through the mud and muck of the rainforest for views of the coast ahead and the mountain range behind us if the weather would clear. I appreciated Bobby's consideration. I knew from experience that he wasn't always this way when his alcohol level dropped. When sober and itching to be anything but, Bobby grew short-tempered and selfish. At those times it was best to keep quiet or vanish all together.

Jack had never been on a horse before, but opted for the larger, more "manly" one, over a smaller, more ride-able horse. The smaller horse also seemed a bit listless. Naturally, that became my horse. One of the sons that lived on the farm at the base of mountain led the pack as we started up the muddy trail, followed by Bobby and Cash, who was still hoping to get laid. I put Jack in front of me, and the second farmhand followed in the rear. We rode single file wearing only bathing suits and shorts with hiking boots, and baseball caps to keep the light rain out off our faces.

The enjoyable and easy ride allowed me plenty of time to once again worry about my passport situation. Would I get it back? Would I have to get a new one made just to leave Costa Rica? If so, would I have time to get the visa stamps I would need to get into China and Mongolia?

I also worried about my horse. She seemed so completely without spirit that I felt she might lie down and die at any moment. I wanted to get off and walk so that she could return to the barn unencumbered by my extra weight, but I chided myself for being silly and overly sensitive. Silently, I nicknamed my horse Listless, and continued my ride up the mountain.

Just short of the top, I rounded a bend in time to see Cash burst up through a narrow chute with a clatter of hooves on the slick uneven rocks.

Safely at the top of the dangerous passage, an unseen Bobby and Cash called down to Jack with words of advice and encouragement. Moments later I watched as Jack and his too large horse stumbled and clattered up the slippery rocks.

Listless and I were next in line. I approached the steep, rocky terrain with confidence in my riding skills, despite the uneasiness of riding a horse that clearly wanted to back in the barn, out of the rain, and be without a rider. As we started up the chute, Listless stumbled. I tucked in to keep our bodies as close as possible. "Come on!" I encouraged. She heaved herself upward, her iron shoes clacking on the mud-slicked uneven rocks.

Suddenly her front hooves were pawing at the air out in front of us and we fell back in to space. I didn't hear a sound. I didn't feel the rain splattering on my upturned face. Instinct kicked in and I let go of the reigns, pushing myself away from Listless as her body fell backward through the sky. We could have been traveling in slow motion. Our bodies arching through the air, with Listless no longer beneath me—but suddenly above me. We landed as one among the rocks and mud at the base of the chute below. I, pinned on my side beneath my horse, the air knocked out of my lungs.

Listless didn't move and I feared she was dead, though my sorrow for her was tempered by the thought that she was still on top of me. "Get. This. Fuh. King. Horse. Off. Of. Me." I grunted as I stretched and grabbed at handfuls of mud in an attempt to drag myself from beneath her.

Gabriel, the farmhand that had been silently following me, leapt off his horse and ran to my aid. He spoke no English, but what could he say? My right leg was securely pinned beneath Listless at a most uncomfortable angle. Jack, in the meantime, was glued to his saddle, unsure of what to do and unable to command his horse to do much anyway. Bobby, up around the bend, heard my fall and returned back down the chute as soon as he could get Cash and Jack out of his way. By then, Gabriel was trying to lift Listless up by the tail so that I could drag my leg out. Clawing at the earth, I pulled and pulled until I could feel my knee and ankle hyper-extending. "Pop!" my leg came free.

I collapsed face down in the mud groaning. This was not a moment for tears. This was a moment for groaning, cursing and rolling in the mud, back and forth, as if to relieve the pain. After a few undignified minutes, I stopped.

Listless suddenly bucked herself back up, clearly shaken from the experience, but still alive. I realized that if she had done that while I was still pinned beneath her, my leg most certainly would have been snapped and several internal organs crushed in the process. I gave her a silent thank you and tried to stand.

My calf had taken the brunt of the fall and was swelling to an impressive circumference, but the bone, while it may have had a hairline fracture, wasn't broken at an uncomfortable angle. The night's rain had softened the ground where Listless and I had landed, leading it to give way under our weight. A pessimist would have cursed God for the rain-slicked, muddy chute, but I silently thanked God for the rain and soft ground and my thin calf. I was just happy to be feeling mostly whole.

Because the path was too narrow and steep for even an ATV, I could either walk or ride Listless back down to the mountain house. Reluctantly, I climbed back on. I now understood the phrase: "Get back up on that horse."

Bobby had a college student, named Jeremy, living at his house for the summer as a houseboy. Jeremy's duties included preventing the place from being robbed or overrun by unwanted guests while he partied away his summer in Costa Rica before returning to law school. Jeremy was a bit of a twit, bowing and kowtowing to Bobby when he was around and whining about him when he wasn't. "Jeremy," Bobby boomed as he arrived back at the house and dismounted from his horse. "Lisa's had a fall. Go get some ice."

Jeremy appeared in the doorway. "Holy shit," he said, and disappeared back into the house.

Bobby and Jack helped me from my horse and onto the couch on the front porch where I had a nice view of the clearing sky. They arranged the damp pillows beneath my leg and made me comfortable. It was clear that I would not be riding down the remainder of the mountain and a half hour into town on an ATV. I wasn't going any farther than the couch; I'd better hope it wasn't broken.

Bobby settled into the chair nearest my head. "You want a drink?" he asked.

"Sure."

"Jeremy! Two rum and cokes!" Bobby called toward the open window, his temper noticeably shorter. Jeremy appeared moments later with a small bag of ice for my leg. "I'll have your drinks out in a minute."

As he handed the bag to me, Bobby asked Jeremy: "Did you use all the ice?"

Jeremy stood staring at my leg. "That's all there was in the freezer," he apologized, his eyes fixated on the huge purple mass that used to be my calf. "You gotta get to a doctor."

With the speed of a hawk diving for supper, Bobby's arm darted in and grabbed the bag of ice before I could set it down on my painful "horse leg."

"Jeremy!" he scolded, handing him the bag of ice. "You *know* I'm an alcoholic. Now go take out some of this ice and put it in my rum and coke."

Well, I thought. At least I forgot about my passport for a while.

HOME, HOME ON THE MONGOLIAN RANGE

I lay on the parched Gobi Desert beneath the wheels of the van hoping I would die. It would be welcome relief from the raging heat both inside and outside my body. But alas, the van was parked and I had wedged into the only sliver of shade for miles that didn't smell overwhelmingly of cooked mutton.

On a healthier day I would have been inside the ger sitting upright, enjoying the relief of the slightly cooler indoors, with a small bottle of soda and another Mongolian feast of mutton and whatever. But right now a flu boiled inside my body, which was taking no prisoners.

We had been on the road all morning, bumping across the scorched desert and stopping whenever my stomach demanded a moment of privacy behind the van. Unfortunately, my "privacy" came with observers: the gear truck following us was only a few dozen yards behind. One would think that in the middle of the Gobi, finding privacy would not be an issue but there I was crouching behind our van to stay out of sight of my fellow travelers—while the driver and luggage assistant in the truck behind us got a full-on view of my backside. I had tried to wave them on for the first few stops but the business at hand demanded immediate attention, and I could only think that after their first horrific sighting they remained behind our van out of duty and simply averted their eyes. I hoped so anyway.

I was in Mongolia to scout out and design a future trip for my clients. It was a chance for me to experience first-hand that which I would send clients to see and do for years to come. Though not always possible, on-site visits are the best way for me to create travel packages that fit the adventure demographic: active, educated, and willing to "suffer" a little to get the most out of a new destination. My clients are not the "blue-haired bus crowd" that many companies package for, and though they are generally well-heeled most are not prima donnas either. My travelers are willing to shell out a few extra bucks to get to unusual or remote places, knowing that rough terrain, uncomfortable lodgings, and language barriers are likely.

I bring it all together for them. I would have to remember to skip this back-of-the-van-exposing-yourself-to-the-locals part of the itinerary for future groups.

I was on this trip with other, let's kindly say, "less adventurous" people in the travel industry—many of whom sold packages to Disney or Las Vegas and just wanted to add another country to their "been there" check-list. Their whining was almost less bearable than my current extreme discomfort. I had neither time nor patience for their complaints about the heat, bumpy roads, and lack of ice for their drinks; besides, I was busy groaning.

Most people assume Mongolia is filled either with raiding remnants of Genghis Khan or camels crossing vast expanses of sand dunes. In fact, it is almost neither. Shaped roughly like an eye surrounded by Russia to the north and China to the south, Mongolia is as diverse in geological features as it is in heritage. In the northwest you'll find heavily forested deep glacial lakes while the vast flat Gobi Desert consumes the south central area. In the north and northeast the plains and hilly highlands are home to the majority of Mongolia's population. With a short visit to the National Museum in Mongolia's capital Ulaanbaatar (more commonly called "UB") you'll discover the distinct clothing once worn by each of the regional tribes further defining cultural boundaries within the country.

This region of Asia has spent most of its time on Earth invading other regions or being invaded, constantly redrawing boundaries while trying to live peacefully. Today, most of the natives have lost their colorful style of dress and their nomadic lifestyle as a result of Russia's recent occupation. A smattering of families living out in the hinterlands and a handful entertainers found in the tourist areas prove exceptions to the rule. It was the former that I sought.

The best way to get to Mongolia is usually via Beijing, where capitalism has a vise-like grip on the hearts of the post-Mao generation. Like alcoholics, they drink in fashion, cell phone technology, material possessions, modern architecture, and travel. This place is *bustling*, and it provides a sharp contrast to Ulaanbaatar with its confetti of ger encampments sprinkled on the outskirts of a gray city featuring crumbling Soviet-era block buildings, centuries-old monasteries, and mediocre western restaurants.

Gers are the traditional home of Mongolians. Don't call them "yurts." Yurta is the Russian word for ger, and Mongolians don't appreciate the insensitive slip of tongue. In fact, a ger is an efficient dwelling that has for centuries allowed the nomads of Central Asia to quickly pick up and move with the seasons or livestock. After removing the thick felt sides from the wooden frame, their ger can be packed onto a few camels or thrown in the back of a yak cart or, more commonly today, a pickup truck.

For the interior layout, one must follow a strict code of design based on Mongolian cosmology: the door always faces south, the woman's side is to the east and the man's to the west. The center is designated for the fire, above which lies a cut-away circle for ventilation covered by a felt flap that can be easily opened or closed by a simple rope system. Along the north wall you will find the hoimor, or home shrine, holding the family's sacred objects. A wooden lattice lines and supports the walls; and the beams that radiate from the center of the ceiling to the walls are always painted in bright red, orange, yellow, blue and green.

In recent years the government in UB, a mix of parliament and president, has decided to drive out the old gers in favor of tasteless cement buildings. Like the American Indians, the government has moved the ger dwellers to restricted "neighborhoods" in the less desirable and more difficult to access outskirts of the city. Their traditional homes appear like bursts of rebellious white flowers in a field of gray cement and brown grass. For most, the plumbing is still outside the home, keeping the inside, where one can find recently slaughtered

meat hanging from support beams, free from the smell and flies common to outhouses. As tourists, we stay in gers and share common bathhouses so that we may enjoy the comforts of western plumbing while experiencing the Mongolian way of life. Our gers rarely have meat hanging from the beams inside.

Right now though, I was enjoying the beauty of the dining ger from the underside of our 1960's style VW van. Directly under the mid-day sun, the scent of mutton in the still, hot air had me holding tightly to my belly while I lay curled in the fetal position. The scalding chrome bumper seared my skin whenever I tried to get deeper into the shade as the shadows moved. Like a monk I chanted my mantra: "Don't throw up, don't throw up, don't throw up."

After lunch, I crawled from under the van to join the others for several more hours of cross-country in-vehicle massages courtesy of the unpaved roadways of remote Mongolia. As we headed east ascending out of the desert, the temperature began to drop and my flu symptoms lessened. I might live after all.

The desert heat gave way to the damp chilly air of the highlands and the unrelenting Gobi sun disappeared behind a sturdy mist that turned air white. We tumbled out of the van and made our way to the gers that we'd each call home for the night. Shivering, I reached into my pack and piled on whatever came out in my hand. I became a kaleidoscope of colors and textures wearing socks for mittens and a t-shirt as a scarf. I didn't care. I would've worn my notebook if I thought it would keep me warm.

While my job is almost non-stop fun and games, it does have a downside. When you finally get to a place as remote as where we now found ourselves in Mongolia, you have to "go with the program" despite any illness, temporary physical handicap, or sock mittens. Time is short and it's likely you may not return again soon. So, while it was alright for me to miss yet another feast of mutton for the luxurious shady underside of the van on our last day in the Gobi, I could not just lay moaning under the warm felt covers waiting for me in my ger if there were still things to do, places to see, or bizarre concoctions to consume.

I trudged to the dining tent for some tea, the thick dampness clinging to my eyelashes and chilling my bones. The locals prefer "salt tea" to our otherwise bland Lipton, and I sipped cautiously. I had been introduced to salt tea in Tibet where the high altitude and smell of rancid yak butter candles had me feeling light-headed for the first few hours, but salt tea (and let's face it, we can chuck yak butter tea into this category as well) is a regional thing akin to Vegemite sandwiches that an

American would likely not concoct at home. People chattered around me as I kept up my mantra: "Don't throw up, don't throw up, don't throw up."

Our hosts had heard that some of us liked horseback riding and they were eager to give us our first experience on Mongolia's shorter and sturdier version of the creatures we have back home. In Mongolia, horses are generally allowed to roam freely so rounding them up takes a certain skill: allow time for someone to run or ride out double, find where the horses are, sneak up on them, lasso one or two, and lead them back. Sure, the horses know what to expect, but that doesn't mean they're going to make it easy. What would take me a lifetime to do once, they do for a group of six in an hour. The Mongolians are proud of their riding heritage and their skills in the "manly arts" which includes a long history of horse rustling as well as wrestling and archery.

The mist lightened as they saddled up our horses and gave us all a "leg up." I was practically in a vertical fetal position with my knees up my nose, the stirrups having been set for the height of an average Mongolian. Vaguely adjusted, we headed out for a nice little ride to the top of a low mountain a few miles off in the distance.

"Yah!" the couple from Colorado flicked their reigns. Positioned in their saddles to take off they looked a bit stunned as their horses continued ambling along. "Yah!" they repeated with a second flick.

"No," our guide instructed, "say 'tchoo'."

"Tchoo!" they sneezed loudly and this time the entire pack took off. The whiner from Michigan squealed and her husband let out a shout of surprise as they discovered this was not going to be your standard-issue American nose-to-butt-we-don't-want-to-be-here trail trudge. Forget tame. Forget everyone fretting about lawsuits. You're on a horse in Mongolia, damn it. Buck up.

"Tchoo!" Kim ordered and raced to the front of the group leaving me between the enthusiastic riders out front and the frightened people behind. Kim, our trip leader and another rider from Colorado, was clearly in her element and having a blast leaving the world behind.

My stirrups felt uncomfortably high and I focused on keeping my center of gravity low, sure that I would go "sproing!" and be launched from my saddle, if I were not vigilant about hunkering down. "Don't throw up don't throw up don't throw up," I chanted to the rhythmic pounding of hooves.

"Tchoo!" I flicked, more a competitive reflex than a desired command. I shot ahead and flew towards the mountain instinctively leaning forward, my calves hugging my horse that clearly wanted to be out front. Oh, this was cool. "Tchoo!" I commanded with more confidence eager to keep up with the Colorado Riders.

We raced across the highlands, the thickening mist blurring my vision. "Woohoo!" we called and laughed and hooted. The freedom was exhilarating. I no longer could hear the complaints of our fat and sedentary traveling companions who had deluded themselves into thinking a trip to Mongolia would be filled with five-star lodges, air-conditioned Cadillacs and cozy Italian restaurants. I no longer felt the desire to curl up and die. I was high on horseback riding in Mongolia. "Woo-Hoooo!!"

My euphoria was occasionally interrupted by a heart-stopping shift in the saddle that would suddenly find me listing to one side. But other than that, and perhaps the cold rain pelting my face, life was good.

By the time we returned, our horses well run and a light sleet falling, the others were in the dining tent awaiting dinner. Our guide pulled the fast riders aside. He would be honored if we would join his family for dinner in their ger.

I had not eaten in more than 24 hours and was shaky from hunger. "Sure!" I enthusiastically accepted, looking forward to a little food.

He beamed. "We will first celebrate your good riding," he said, "with traditional fermented camels milk."

At least it wasn't mutton.

A SUMMIT
CELEBRATION OF SORTS

A severe asthma attack would have sounded better. Huddled in the dark, I gasped for air while Bongo chatted like we were at a cocktail party. I had no idea what he was saying; I just wanted to catch my breath.

Below me I could hear Carol and Ann, two sisters in my group, encouraging each other upwards. Just above my shoulder George, the least affected of us, was also breathing hard. Next to him sat Bongo's brother and our lead guide, Kennedy, who didn't seem bothered by the lack of oxygen, icy wind or grit that now coated our teeth and insides of our noses. Somewhere in the night, far below us, Mike slept snuggled in his sleeping bag at High Camp, a comfortable 15,800 feet above sea level. He had talked himself out of reaching the summit before he ever left high camp knowing he would never stand on the Roof of Africa. I wasn't so sure that I'd make it to the summit either, though I was expending much more effort in the process.

"Do you know where you are?" Bongo asked.

"I think I'm in hell," I tried to sound cheerful.

"No! Last year, where I said, 'Keep going guys. You are close to the top now.' That is here."

"Bongo," I reminded him, "I had bronchitis and was practically coughing up blood." How could I forget?

This was a cakewalk compared to last year's summit attempt. Last year we started with a group of twelve. Four nights later only eight set out for the summit of Kilimanjaro, two having turned back on the second day, and two choosing to stay in their tents at the high camp Barafu, just above 15,000 feet. When the last of us had dragged into Barafu that night it was a chaotic mess as several groups had arrived from different access trails in preparation for a summit attempt. Tents from the different groups were intermixed causing confusion and stress for all. Many had never spent time a vertical mile higher than most ski slopes on the planet. The camp felt like walking through a MASH unit: some

people crying in their tents from exhaustion and others throwing up whenever the moment inspired them, not bothered by etiquette or hazardous placement. It was a minefield of vomit. We nicknamed the camp BARFu and I swore my groups would never stay there again.

Last year, of the eight that set out for the summit, I was one of the three who didn't make it, having turned back somewhere far into the night as blasts of wind hit the 50 miles per hour mark. At about 120 pounds and 5'10" I felt like a sail catching the icy air as it raged off the summit glacier trying to sweep down everything in its pathway.

Surprisingly, I didn't cough as I trudged up the steep slope of scree. I was focused on my routine of breathe-in-step-step-breathe-out, breathe-in-step-step-breathe-out. But I often had to stop either to regain my footing, as the gravel-size scree would slip away beneath each step, or to catch my breath from the exertion against the wind. That was when I would start coughing. It would burn deep in my lungs and persist until my head was on the verge of exploding. Though I was essentially over the bronchitis that had hit me three weeks earlier, the air was so thin above 18,000 feet that the struggle to breathe ended in moist coughing fits that sounded like the start of pulmonary edema. At high altitude people die from pulmonary edema; I preferred to call mine "mountaineer's hack."

Worse still, that night the moon had set more than an hour earlier and dawn still hung under the horizon. My headlamp battery was long since dead, and I was exhausted from battling the wind. I gave plenty of thought to my situation, creating a mental list of pros and cons. As group leader they didn't need me to make it to the summit – that's what the guides were for. Go down. I could always try again another year with a future group. Go down. My clients didn't need me to develop pulmonary edema and die, ruining their trip and putting an unhappy ending on the story of their African adventure. Go down.

On the other hand, I had argued with myself as I heaved my body against the wind and tried to keep my feet beneath me, making it to the summit was a matter of personal pride. Go up. I'm a mountaineer and a group leader, damn it – I can hack (no pun intended) the discomfort. Go up. The mountain says, *See Me, I'm Worthy.* Go up.

Worthy of *what* exactly is a personal thing. Does my ego require it? I asked myself. Go down.

And so a year ago, hunkered down against an angry glacial wind in a coughing fit that left tears freezing in the corners of my eyes, my group scattered on the trail to the summit crowded with icicle-covered zombies, I made the decision to turn myself around and return to Barfu choosing good sense over ego. Bongo tried to convince me that

I was very close but he had a habit of shortening distances and times – significantly. Ultimately, he returned to camp with me, making sure I found my tent in the wind-battered vomit-splattered bedlam. I crawled into my sleeping bag as the early morning sun crested over Mawenzi Peak and heated my tent to a toasty 50 degrees. Though the wind beat the sides of my tent like a drum, I was warm and lying down and only coughing occasionally. I didn't even taste blood any more.

With access to more than 3,000 vertical feet of additional oxygen, my head and lungs began to clear and I began to question my decision. Maybe I really was that close. Maybe Bongo was telling me the truth. Maybe... maybe... maybe... Somehow, I drifted off to sleep.

The year had passed quickly and I'd had many opportunities to consider my decision. As I sat on Heartbreak Hill I realized I must have been much closer to the summit than I had believed a year ago. Admittedly, I had long ago lost faith in Bongo's ability to estimate time and distances. The standard joke in our group was: How much further, Bongo? Two hours. It was always the same reply whether we were four hours or twenty minutes from our destination. We were on African Time.

"How far?" I asked.

"Just there."

"Don't lie to me, Bongo."

"It's true guys. Just there."

"Two hours?"

"Nooo. Come on guys," he said to only me, knowing that I was teasing him, but still confused on how to use the English word 'guy.'

"Promise?"

"Yeah, sure. It's true guys."

I could hear George and Kennedy talking in the dark and see the sisters below me with their headlamps shining on their packs as they replaced their nearly frozen water and snack food. The wind blew mildly compared to a year ago, and there were no crowds this year. Tonight the brilliant full moon allowed us to climb without using our headlamps. It was, in short, a beautiful night of exhausting labor toward an exciting destination. I had dreamt about it for a year. Working out with a backpack full of bricks, I envisioned myself on the summit as the departure date drew near. And this year I had stayed away from sick people.

Now I mused, what would I do when I finally got there? On one hand, I expected to cry with joy; on the other hand a shout of exhilaration was in order. Perhaps I would do both, a sobbing hooting combination that would better express all the emotion I had stored up for the summit. No, wait. I think I'll drop on all fours and kiss the ground. Okay, I'll kiss the ground while weeping thankfully and possibly whoop with delight....

I ripped open a Power Gel contemplating the nearness of success. Just there. "Bleah…" I gagged. This stuff was awful: pure sugar goo in a tropical fruit flavor I could not identify. How did people consume these things without throwing up? I was hungry and tired but was this gel really the answer?

Rested and determined to continue, I said to Bongo, "Let's go," and bit down on the packet, holding it in my teeth. I would just "sip" it to give myself strength on the final push.

I stood, grabbed my pack, and was off. I was going to the summit. It was just there. I could do this. Just there. In my mind, I was the Little Engine That Could, puffing and steaming towards the top. Each step a chug. Chug…chug…chug… chug.

Surprised, the others rose and followed. The pink tint of dawn was on the horizon, the air an opaque deep blue. The long, black, cold, miserable night was now behind us, Stella Point ahead. Just there. Chug…chug…chug…chug. Each step slipped on the scree. One step up, one half step down, but I didn't care. I was going to the summit. First stop: Stella Point. "Stellllllllla!" I did my best *Streetcar Named Desire* impression with a packet of goo clenched in my front teeth. "Stellllllllllla!"

As a volcanic cone, Kilimanjaro has a long rim line, all of which is considered "the top." Once you hit Stella Point, the most accessible point on the rim via the Machame Route, you officially earn a green certificate showing that you've reached the top. From Stella, however, you still have a 45-minute walk and another 400' feet of elevation gain to get to the true summit: Uhuru.

Freedom. What a beautiful Swahili word.

Climbers who make it to Uhuru get a gold certificate and can take their photo next to a sign proving that they were there, that they made it to the Roof of Africa. All 19,345 vertical feet are now below them. Climbers who get to Stella Point and turn back get to take their picture next to an unidentified rock. They need the certificate to show that all their walking ended in some tangible item of success.

Chug…chug…chug…chug. I was lightheaded and tunnel vision had set in, the blast of exertion requiring more oxygen than I could get into my blood stream as I sucked air in around the disgusting packet wedged in my teeth.

I forged on. Chug…chug…chug…chug.

To my fellow climbers below, I did not look like the Little Engine That Could. I looked like a drunk, slipping and stumbling and yelling the only phrase most people recognize from that damn Tennessee Williams play. They rose and followed if for no other reason than to see if I had gone mad. The crowds of the previous year were gone and it was just us right here, right now. Others climbed below us and people ascended a different route that would intersect with ours at Stella Point; but here on Heartbreak Hill, the interminable scree-slipping steep shoulder on the tallest mountain on the African continent, we were alone. And I intended to get off that cursed piece of land alive.

Through the deep blue air, I could myopically make out what appeared to be a big rock up only another 20 or 30 vertical feet ahead. That was a good sign, wasn't it? I pressed on. Chug...chug...chug...chug. My vision stayed dangerously narrow, my heart bursting in my chest, the inside of my nose chapped and raw from the air I sucked in, that disgusting tropical goo oozing into my mouth. I was either going to make it or die.

And suddenly, I reached the apex of Heartbreak Hill and tipped over to flatter ground. I was on the rim! "Stelllllla!!" My eyes welled with tears and I dropped to kiss the ground. The packet of goo fell from my mouth. I bent over... and threw up.

It took me by complete surprise. *Puke* was not in my celebration plan. Yet, there I was, on all fours heaving out every last bit of tropical yuck without an ounce of concern for etiquette or location.

Reaching the summit of Kilimanjaro produces a storm of emotions that you really can't prepare for. You've been hiking up and down high altitude ridges for days, pawing your way through fields of scree, stumbling along in whipping sleet that stings your face and blurs your vision, fighting off dehydration and hunger and headaches, and tolerating companions you hope never to see again once you pick up your luggage at your home airport. Ever.

But you stick to it, this vertical marathon, and you can now see the finish line. All negative thoughts vanish. You suddenly remember the radiant beauty of the summit glacier at night crowned by a million sparkling stars, and jubilantly recall free climbing the Lava Towers at 15,000 feet. You hold tightly to the memory of waking to steaming hot tea brought to your tent each morning by an always-cheerful cook's assistant, and chatting for hours on the trail with your companions, your friends.

At Stella Point, I am on my knees, having heaved up the small amount of never-to-cross-my-lips-again tropical goo. Elation and exhaustion course through my system as my fellow climbers arrive and circle around me. My vision broadens and my breathing slows back to manageable. I look up at Bongo who offers me his hand. "How much further?" I smile.

"Just two hours, guys."

THE TRUTH ABOUT LENTICULAR CLOUDS

While I'm certain that at least one science teacher during my school years must have mentioned it, the first time I actually remember hearing about lenticular clouds I was mountaineering in the Rockies on a five day trip with two guys I barely knew. The plan was to camp at Goblins Forest on Longs Peak at night and work on rope techniques and technical skills in Estes Park with our guide, Bruce, during the days. On our last day of practice before we'd attempt a technical ascent of Longs Peak, the classic "14er" in nearby Rocky Mountain National Park, I found myself almost hugging a wall of ice about sixty feet above the ground.

On this rather fine afternoon I was ascending a vertical snow wall using ice axes. "Can you see those clouds?" Bruce called down to me.

They were hard to miss. Like a couple of spaceships from a bad 1950s sci-fi movie these clouds, like smooth-edged dinner plates with dome centers, had gathered over some peaks to the southwest of us. "Cool," I said and thunked my right ice axe up another arm's length.

I really liked this ice climbing stuff. With complete faith in the belay rope and summer soft snow ice to climb, I was a Spiderwoman without the blue tights. I transferred my weight to check that the pick, with its large saw-like teeth, was solidly placed. Thunk! I moved the other pick up to matching height. Kick! Up went the right boot, driving the nose spikes of my crampons into the softened snow ice. Transfer weight to the right boot and kick! I brought the left boot up to matching height, ready to start the cycle again. Like climbing a rope with jumars and foot loops, once you got the rhythm—and assuming no physical roadblocks—you can make steady progress without flailing about or burning up all your energy. Thunk!

"I don't see any clouds," Mike calls from beneath me.

"You have to get higher!" we call back down to him.

Moments later I topped out and stood above the ice cliff looking down on my two climbing partners. Mike had already attempted to summit Longs Peak twice and was determined to make it this time. He said on his last attempt he hiked with his girlfriend, driving straight to the Park from the airport and immediately starting to climb. Though they were hiking the non-technical "Keyhole" Route he became ill around 12,000 feet, and they quit at the Boulder Field below the keyhole. For reasons I wasn't quite clear on, Mike blamed his now ex-girlfriend.

In truth, once a person ascends above 7000 feet they can start to feel the effects of altitude. The trailhead for Longs is at 9,400 feet so many people already don't feel well before they leave their cars. Altitude sickness comes in a variety of forms, including everything from "general malaise" to physical illness. I've seen people get grouchy. I've seen people cry. I've stepped around more than my share of landmines deposited from either end of climbers who have developed digestive issues. And then of course, there are the headaches. Temple squeezing, vision blurring, nausea inducing clangs that hammer with each heartbeat are the most troublesome, but the less violent headaches can be just as debilitating depending on the climber's determination to reach the summit.

Many inexperienced climbers have a blissfully ignorant idea of what it takes to climb in the Rockies. After all, none of these peaks are the world's highest, so how hard can it be?? In fact, only about 30 percent of the people who attempt Longs make it to the summit.

The Rockies eat people. The first to go are the ones who arrive in t-shirts and shorts because they are hiking in the summer. *Oh, yeah, as if it's going to snow*, they say. *Come on, it's July!* But snow in the upper elevations of the Rockies knows no seasonal boundaries and so the day-trippers suddenly find themselves shivering in freezing rain or snow, the smart ones making a beeline for lower elevations.

The next to go are the ones who race for the summit—often driven by ego—when they have not allowed their bodies to properly acclimate. This is especially common with people like Mike who fly in from the flatlands and decide they are going to get up to the summit and back down for a late dinner. Generally, the optimism and energy that they have in the first couple hundred feet of elevation gain drains away in the lower switchbacks and is replaced with misery of the aforementioned sorts by the time they reach tree line. It's a real shot to the ego to be trudging along on the slope and have a local runner jog past going uphill and hardly sweating.

Finally, there are those who just can't heed

good advice. Those are the people who are struck by lightening or freeze to death because they've pushed on when all the warning indicators have been telling them to go back. Some of the warning signs are verbal:

Heed the weather reports.

Be off the summit of Longs by 11am.

Some are visual: Always watch the sky...

But even heeding good advice doesn't guarantee you'll stay ahead of the weather.

I had a group climbing the Keyhole Route one summer and had given strict instructions for turnaround times from different points on the backside of Longs based on the weather forecast and how quickly one should climb or how well one should feel. Starting at the back of the pack I made three women turn around within an hour or two whom I knew would not make it and would require as long to descend to the Boulder Field as it would take to go up. Continuing on, I got the last of the slow climbers onto the summit, photographed and heading back down by 11am, our designated turn-around time. I had barely given myself a mental pat on the back when I realized we were far from finished.

The last climber to summit turned out to be borderline terrified on the slabs, a section in "The Homestretch" that angles sharply toward the peak for about three hundred vertical feet at an elevation mostly above 14,000 feet. When dry, the Homestretch, which requires occasional hand scrambles over loose rock and thoughtful placement of your feet, was more frightening to consider than to actually climb across and down. My straggler was giving the large angled slabs great consideration and his fear of sliding off the side of the mountain increased with each tentative step. He went from hiking down to crab walking sideways, leaning forward with his hands on the slabs for balance, to finally scooching on his butt. Our painfully slow progress and his new body position gave us a terrific opportunity to watch the storm move in. "Come on!" I yelled and grabbed his hand, yanking him upright. "There's no time for sliding down on your butt. Get moving!"

An hour later I was still driving him like a mule along rocky ledges and steep runs with names like The Narrows and The Trough. This job gets a little weird at times.

The rain and lightening swooped down the range and we were now part of a skinny drip of climbers hustling single-file for the Keyhole. We had caught up to our oldest climber, a good twenty years older than "Pokey" when we felt the first few drops of rain. Thankfully, the balance of our group was through the Keyhole and descending to the Boulder Field where our small huddle of tents welcomed yellow and blue dots, another several hundred-foot scramble directly below. The icy water hit the back of my neck. "Come on, guys... Move!" I yelled.

The problem with the Keyhole, which is really more of a notch than a hole, is that only one person can reasonably get through it at a time and there was already a line of about ten climbers waiting to cross over. Pokey finally made it to the front of the line as the snow began to fall. The mix of snow and lightening was a fascinating show better watched from a safe distance, which would not include our present position on a wet ridge in the strike zone.

A few college students from Denver hunkered down shivering in the line behind us in t-shirts and shorts, freezing and cussing as my client struggled with his fears and his footing. In the few minutes that it took him to get through the slick passage a thick snow had begun to fall.

The snow and gusting winds made sticking on the steep rocky slope a bit tricky and I nearly flung myself through the Keyhole to keep the line moving as still another dozen or so people behind me waited to get through. Another fifty feet below we piled into a small shelter built of rocks and named after Agnes Vaille who died in a sudden storm back in the early 1900s. The shelter, built in 1927, is now on the National Register of Historic Places. More and more climbers piled into the shelter until we were proverbial sardines, packed shoulder to shoulder, some even standing on benches to make room for more, and all grateful for the collective body heat. I gave silent thanks to Agnes. Her death had probably saved thousands of lives over the past three-quarters of a century.

We finished that climb, the group intact and uninjured, with the last of the hikers arriving exhausted to the parking lot around 5pm. I'm quite sure that for some it was the first and last of Colorado's fifty-two 14ers that they would ever climb. For others, like Pokey, the elation of conquering one's fears would lead to more climbs. I had to give the guy credit. Veni, vidi, vici.

Now as we stood at the top of our ice cliff, Bruce explained to me how cloud formations tell you pretty specific and reliable information. "A sky full of puffball clouds means you're going to get some form of precipitation, generally in 6 – 12 hours" he said. "Lenticular clouds, on the other hand, warn of high winds and precipitation, often arriving within the next few hours – especially at higher elevations."

I tried to recall the clouds the morning of our group summit. I drew a blank. "Think we'll get snow up on Longs tomorrow?" I asked, coiling my climbing rope. It was heavy and wet from the snowmelt.

"Sure," Bruce replied. "Summer snow

storms are common on Longs. People get trapped in them all the time."

I told him the story of my group as DJ, the 6' 2" Texan with $1500 of new equipment topped out and we helped him over the edge. Bruce commiserated saying that each summer he found himself exposed to storms in the Rockies due to slow clients. "It's even worse," he said, "on technical climbs when you're hanging against the face or slipping on the slabs near the summit and a climber becomes paralyzed with fear."

DJ now stood beside me. An easy-going guy eager to learn and experience mountaineering, DJ was still a little surprised to find himself here. Only a few weeks earlier DJ met Mike while rollerblading on the lakefront as part of one of the many clubs that bloom in the parks during summer in Chicago. He was easily talked into joining us. About that same time, my girlfriend cancelled and suddenly I was the "odd (wo)man out." Within days DJ was shepherded around REI as Mike loaded up his cart with the latest technical gear, "must have" stuff that he might never use again. He took it all in stride and handed over his credit card – after all, isn't that what eBay was for?

I could hear Mike making his way up the ice cliff. He complained noisily about his expensive equipment causing him difficulties and slowing his ascent, giving me the sense that Mike often found fault with external things—equipment, people, situations—instead of with himself. Not getting to the top first was clearly an issue for him. We could hear him grumbling loudly over the edge though neither DJ nor I considered it a race.

Whatever. I was much more into the cloud thing.

The spaceships seemed to hover over the top of the peaks, their smooth sides curved by the force of the wind. As Mike topped out he stopped his complaining, awed by the unusual formations. "So that's what you guys have been looking at."

Bruce repeated his telltale cloud signs to the guys as we packed up our gear. "I think we're going to have to get an even earlier start tomorrow," he said. "Plan to leave the Boulder Field at about 3 or 3:30am."

"It doesn't look very threatening," Mike said.

"Are you planning to camp up there with us?" I asked.

"I can't. There's a 4th of July party tonight and all the guides get together on rafts and float down during the fireworks. It's a riot! Total whitewater in parts."

"Don't spill your beer," I smiled.

"Never!"

So Bruce was going to go party, where he'd probably get no sleep, and then start hoofing up the blackened trail – roughly 6 miles to the Boulder Field – with a fully loaded pack in the wee hours of the night. Impressive.

DJ, Mike and I returned to Goblins Forest, packed up our gear, and headed for the Boulder Field. I left my single-person tent back in the car so that we'd have less weight to shuttle up, having now the additional weight of soggy ropes, double plastic mountaineering boots, harnesses and carabineers. My pack was easily 55 pounds with water, food, sleeping bag, Thermarest, and shared equipment. I shouldered my burden without whining, cinched up my padded hip belt, and started my slow hike.

Longs Peak is a terrific hike, the lower elevations filled with fields and forests giving way to open tundra and scenic stops at the higher elevations. Though it is only an elevation gain of about ½ mile from Goblins Forest to the Boulder Field, many people are woozy to start with and feel miserable by the time they've made it to 12,400 feet. One way to keep the misery to a minimum is to hike slowly. For me this was easy—my heavy pack felt like I was giving a piggyback ride to Sasquach.

Mike, on the other hand, was soothing his self-inflicted bruised ego by hustling up the trail to show us that he didn't consider his pack heavy. And quite honestly, since he was diligent in loading up DJ and I with group gear, he probably car-

ried the same amount of weight as me though he was 40 pounds heavier, and presumably stronger. Whatever.

DJ and I chatted and kept an even pace, stopping for shelter beneath a garage-sized boulder during a brief rainstorm. We reached our destination, the far end of Boulder Field, to find that Mike was already there and pitching the tent. He apparently felt quite smug. Ok, you win. I was just happy to off-load my pack.

Inside our tent we laid out our sleeping bags, strategically putting DJ between Mike and I because I was feeling less and less tolerant toward him and his litany of whines and complaints, this time featuring gastrointestinal issues and a headache. The former was potent enough for us to open the tent door and window flap to allow the wind to blow through and hopefully keep the inside gas level to something less than explosive. The latter was not enough to keep Mike from handing out assignments like we were his personal support staff. "DJ, go get water." "Lisa, make dinner."

"Mike, kiss my..." I thought but kept my lip buttoned. We still had another 24 hours together. I blissfully thought: thank god he's not a client.

After a hot meal Mike was happier and slightly more bearable. When I saw him take a stack of magazines and a book from the bottom of his pack though, I almost went ballistic. He had made me leave my small writing journal behind because it was "unnecessary extra weight" and he didn't want to carry any additional gear that would be displaced from my pack because of my journal. With five pounds of reading material in the bottom of his pack it meant that DJ and I were subject to carrying *his* extra weight!

I had to get out of there. I set off on a late afternoon hike to explore the area, scrambling up to the edge overlooking the Diamond. The Diamond is a sheer, technical, multi-pitch rock climb where one can't help but feel amazed and very tiny as you visually scour the surface in search of fearless individuals making their way up a 600-meter face. Climbers on the 5th pitch near the top can look back over their shoulder and spot the very blue Chasm Lake below, seemingly puddle-size. I could sit and marvel at the strength and tenacity of these climbers for hours, especially the crazy ones in the bivvy sacks suspended midway up the Diamond and ready for a night's sleep.

Looking off in the other direction I had a great view of Storm Peak, an accessible pile of rocks with a summit at 13,326 feet considered a reasonable alternative for people unable to get to the summit of Longs before bad weather kicks in. With my back to the Diamond I could also see the valley where, as darkness began to settle, fireworks displays from several different towns burst into the air *below* me.

I picked my way back down to the tent, having regained my composure and decided to take a very Zen-like approach to my relationship with Mike. "I'm just not going to let him bother me," I smiled to myself as the sky lit up with a million white stars.

"Well, Bruce must not know what he's talking about," Mike said upon my arrival. "There's not a cloud in the sky, let alone any rain or snow."

I simply raised my eyebrow and headed off to brush my teeth with some icy cold mountain water. I noted that Mike was correct – there wasn't a cloud in the sky at the moment—but I had full confidence that if Bruce said the spaceship clouds were lenticular and lenticular clouds foretell high winds and precipitation, then it must be so. Teeth clean, with nothing to read and no journal to write in, I quickly fell asleep.

Three a.m. came quickly and I was roused out of a deep and wonderful slumber. I saw Bruce outside with his headlamp shining in. "Let's go! Rise and shine climbers!" he called in to us. I dragged myself from my warm and cozy sleeping bag, pulled on my outer clothes, and set the water to boil outside. In the black stillness DJ and I ate oatmeal, mine from a beat up thermal mug with a blue plastic spoon shivering in my gloved hand.

My gloves are old, black, woolen things I grabbed without looking at. After I pulled them on I discovered two fingers on each hand had holes at the tip. Oh well, at least they're even. Bruce munched on a PowerBar and chided Mike to pick up the pace.

Mike had apparently not felt or slept well all night. He was slow to dress. He whined and complained, unable to find the necessary gear. He was slow to eat. I thought he was suffering from a bout of bad karma in addition to his altitude sickness so I said nothing. An hour later he was finally ready. We secured the tent fly, turned, and took our first steps through Boulder Field toward the steep snowfield on the North Face. I was so excited! "This is going to be a blast!" I thought.

And then, an icy rain began to fall.

*   *   *

Early October the following year I will find myself at a scenic overlook in Yosemite with a few friends. At this scenic viewpoint we will stop, and in storm force winds we will take photos of each other laughing with our hair blowing wildly back and whipping around our heads into knots. I will point out to my friends the lenticular clouds I see and explain how I learned that these clouds predict wind and snow at higher elevations, like where we are on the Pass in Yosemite. I'll tell them that Mike did not believe clouds could predict the weather until we were at 14,000' on a technical climb in a July snowstorm, hugging a crag in the granite on the North Face with frozen rain cascading down and into the holes in my glove tips. A storm—I will emphasize—was predicted by clouds, just like the ones we were now looking at.

My visual warning will be poo-poohed ("See," I'm told, "It's all wind and no snow.") and we will drive over the Pass to Mono Lake to view and photograph its strange salt formations and visit its museum. As we cross the Pass we will be warned that the Park Service may close it for the season due to snow that is expected to fall. We'll say thank you and wave a friendly good-bye, determined to ignore the verbal warning as well, and continue on our way.

While we're over there, we'll also stop for a hike in Tuolomne Meadows where we'll walk for an hour or so, stopping for more photographs including one of us standing with arms over each other's shoulders at a trail sign, and another by a babbling brook where we'll marvel at the gentle, soft, beautiful snow that has begun to fall.

Some time later we'll get back to the parking lot littered with broken glass from bears smashing their ways into cars for food left behind by tourists who think the bears will not smell their half-eaten bag of Doritos if they just hide it under the driver's seat. The parking lot is proof where non-believers change their tune when *their* car windows are reduced to glittery rubble, *their* car seats get shredded and disgorged, and they're faced with *their* outrageous rental car repair bill. When we arrive, the lot will be all white, the forest green bear-proof dumpster and our rental car white mounds breaking the smooth snow lot surface. We'll have to brush off almost two inches of heavy snow to clear our windows for the ride home.

And then, by the time we reach the Pass—the gateway to our cabin on the other side of the Park—we'll find ourselves in a long line of cars all being turned back. "What do you mean 'go around'? It's a twelve-hour drive!" we'll exclaim through windows rolled down only a few inches to keep the snow from blowing in. "At least." the Ranger will reply. His look says: "We told you not to cross the Pass." I roll up the window as the magnitude of the situation sets in.

We will then spend the next 12 hours trying to drive our tiny snow-coated car without chains. A joke in the continuing thick snowstorm that's piling drifts and making the treacherous narrow road a frightening vague gray ribbon with mashed potato piles of snow squished out from beneath tires. We are turned back at each successive Pass we start to drive up, directed to continue around the Park.

Finally, risking our three lives and perhaps countless others I will follow a semi carrying fuel as it climbs a Pass miles and miles and miles away from where we need to be. I will smile and wave to the police person or park ranger who looks part snowman and who is trying to stop me and turn me back, slowly grinding forward, occasionally slipping, occasionally stopping my own heart. I glance through my snow-covered window at the precipice off to my left. There is nothing but death out there.

The steady thump-thump-thump of the windshield wipers mimic the beat of my heart, which I can feel more in my throat than in my chest. I will stay in low gear, giving it enough gas to keep moving forward at a steady pace. If I have to stop we will start sliding backward and there is nothing good back there. I see brake lights ahead of me and slow the trickle of gas even more. Not a one of us is speaking. Not a one of us is even breathing. And then I come to a stop.

We do not slide backwards, but as soon as I touch the accelerator again the back of the car skids to the left. We all inhale sharply. I let off the gas and straighten the front wheels to drive forward, though "forward" at this moment in time takes me directly into the side of the cliff wall. I give it the slightest touch of gas and we roll through the heavy snow. Each one of us has a hand on our door handle, ready to pull and release ourselves onto the snowy ground should the car decide to fly off the road and over the cliff. I slowly arc a turn and center the car behind the gas truck.

I gotta pee. And then I think, "Yeah, as if that's going to happen for another three hours." I'm not sure this is a welcome distraction, but once the thought has crossed my mind it's there to stay.

I creep forward with the speed of a sloth. "Don't die. Don't kill your friends. Please Mr. Truck Driver, don't slide backward."

A lifetime passes with each minute. I want to yell at my friends. On the other hand, we did have a fun day—if we live to tell the story...

A few hours later we will finally be back at our cottage. Tired, hungry, cold, and a wee bit irritated I will wonder: Why does no one believe it when they're told the truth about lenticular clouds???

Whatever happened to you, Mike, Bruce, and DJ?

Just between us: The answer is that...

...We abandoned the climb near the summit, hunkered down on slabs slicked with sleet, icy rainwater running in through the holes in my black woolen gloves. Mike had crossed the line between bearable and intolerable, his complaints seemingly more a response to fear and altitude sickness. Still roped together we turned around, DJ taking the lead back toward the Boulder Field. Plunge-stepping down the steep snowfield in the freezing rain DJ takes a step that falls away beneath his foot. "Augh! Falling!" he called, startled. I turned to face the summit, threw myself onto my ice axe, the adz digging into the soft snow as I feel the rope yank my waist. "Self arrest!" I yell up toward Mike and Bruce. And then I am dragged with increasing speed down the mountain. Below me DJ gives a whoop and though I am doing my best to dig in, kicking my toes into the snow to stop our accelerating slide toward the massive collection of large and jagged boulders where the snow ends, a whoop escapes my lips as well. Suddenly we are laughing out loud, yelling "self arrest!" and kicking our toes and jamming our ice axes into the too forgiving snow. I know I should be serious but DJ and I are no longer adults. We are suddenly kids again, laughing as the soft snow flies up around us and jams up into our jackets. By the time we stop we are ready to jump up and do it again, but we compose ourselves and stand up, do a quick safety check and continue our plunge steps. Later, we laugh again about the riotous ride down the snowfield and Mike, feeling left out will claim that he saved us from certain death, using the proper arrest technique.

OK, Mike. Whatever.

MEETING THE MOUNTAIN MOAI

K O sat with the map on her knees, head down, studying the thin line we had followed into the mountains of central Chile. "I think just ahead the road goes dot, dot, dot then stops," she said. "Why don't we just park at the end of the road and start hiking from there?"

I, driving our tiny white "Pop" car (think: Geo Metro with a silly name) up into the Andes, had been negotiating the curves of this narrow mountain road with an unusually high volume of on-coming semi trucks. "What the..." I thought. "Where are these things coming from?" As I contemplated what on this mountain required so many semis with black canvas-covered trailers, I realized we might have greater concerns.

69

"KO," I said, "I just passed a sign with two crossed guns."

As I completed another curve to the left, KO looked up from the map; I stomped on the brakes just in time, avoiding smashing through the gate that blocked our passage. AK-47s snapped down from both sides as men in drab green military attire swarmed our car. I got a sickening feeling these guys weren't up here to squirrel hunt.

"Ho-Ly shit!" I breathed. We froze, staring through the windshield at the sight before us. We turned to look at each other, eyes as big as pie plates. We burst out laughing.

*   *   *

KO and I met several years ago through ski racing and had become fast friends. Under the guise of skiing, we had visited several places around the globe, but our dream of hitting the slopes in South America had remained on the "To Do" list until a few weeks ago, when we decided to burn off some frequent flyer miles and see what the other hemisphere held. With an October departure, we knew we were in for late spring ski conditions but we didn't care—we'd happily ski down a pile of broken glass just to get our boards beneath our feet again.

On our arrival in Chile, we negotiated the feeding frenzy of cabbies that descended on the influx of fresh meat, and changed dollars for pesos at the cambio. Eventually we found ourselves safely ensconced in a small property near the foot of a mountain in the center of Santiago. The Foresta Hotel was filled with dark wood, blood-red velvet, and a staff that spoke little English. We were given a tiny room above the noisy street where we dropped our bags and spread out a map and newspaper.

The snow reports listed crummy late season conditions with wet snow and bare patches, so we opted to put off skiing until later in the trip, filling our days with sightseeing, hiking, and perhaps rafting or wine tasting. We tramped up Cerro Santa Lucia, strolled in the park along the river and visited museums and historical sites. The city bustled with a European style I had not expected. The transportation system was as efficient, and roadways as clogged, as any self-respecting metropolis in the U.S. We immediately loved this place.

We generously improved the economy in the open-air markets where locals hawked everything from fruit and fish to hand-woven hats and woolen sweaters. At the "super mercados" that were taking over — massive warehouses haloed with glaring overhead lights that sold everything from underwear to imported sausages — we

71

picked up a few staples and hurried out. Apparently capitalism and mass consumption were alive and kicking in Chile.

Santiago sits like a pearl in the heart of this string bean country that, if laid over the U.S., would stretch from the northwestern tip of Washington State to the far southeastern end of Florida. Take a leisurely drive about two hours west and you'll find yourself on the sunny coast; drive two hours east and you'll find yourself suddenly gasping for air at 10,000 feet in the Andes. The north end of the country hosts the high-altitude Atacama Desert. In the south lies the famous Patagonia, shared with Argentina, where pack animals and hikers roam unencumbered by schedules or showers amidst towering glaciers and wind carved peaks.

In short, Chile is a country so long and narrow and diverse that two weeks would not allow any reasonable traveler to do it justice. We decided to focus our energies on one region at a time.

For starters, we chose to stay central. This would give us a chance to get to know the capital, Santiago, as well as the central coast, the Andes, and the wineries in-between. We would have to return another time for the famed Lake District, a short flight to the south, where the number-one pastime is fly-fishing in the pristine rivers that snake through a landscape heaving with volcanoes. A third visit would allow us to hike Patagonia, and a fourth trip to Chile would cover the northern desert and mysterious Easter Island with its enormous Moais, men of stone, that stand silent guard over a piece of land that lies several hours flight from the continental shore.

In Chile, dialects are so thick that people from one region can't understand people from another region. Forget about effectively communicating with high school level American Spanglish. After two days of mangling their language with strained facial gestures for emphasis, I was confident enough to venture out of the city. We approached the concierge at the Hyatt for assistance with hiring a rental car. "Hola. Necessito un carro," I blurted, skipping any attempt at formality or graciousness. "Ah, yes," he replied in perfect English, "the Hertz office is down that corridor to the right."

"Thank you," I blushed.

The rental agent turned out to be my Spanish language soul mate. He struggled with English as much as I struggled with Spanish. Thus began the tri-lingual charades that would continue throughout our trip. I would start by torturing some perfectly reasonable phrase in Spanish with a look of great earnestness. We would then listen intently to the response and try to discern the meaning by flipping through our Spanish-English dictionary and using KO's more extensive French vocabulary (she made it to French V in high school). Team America would then huddle for a brief debate and plan our response, which I would attempt again, aided by ridiculous hand and facial gestures.

During our two weeks in Chile, this tag team communication system had netted us a meal of grilled innards of Lord Knows What, a $40 charge for common bottled water over a single dinner, plenty of looks of consternation and most often, unplanned group conversations filled with laughter at our expense. Occasionally we would even get what we thought we asked for. So, for the most part, it was working wonderfully.

* * *

Now we just had to figure out how to invite the stone-faced-gun-toting mountain militia to play "Guess What The Idiot Americans Are Trying To Say" before we ended up dead.

Laughter, even as unplanned and short-lived as ours, is not recommended when a dozen AK-47s are pointing at your head as you sit in a little white Fred Flintstone mobile in a remote part of some mountain range. Unfortunately, our spontaneous reaction was all we could muster without actually peeing in our pants. I suddenly regretted not telling anyone where we were going.

Their faces remained emotionless; their

guns at the ready. Maybe we wouldn't have to go
to Easter Island to see the Moais after all. Not
one for sitting around waiting to be shot, I seized
the moment. Putting on my most non-threatening
smile, I leaned out my window with the map in my
hand. "Hi! I think we're lost. Can you help us?"

The Moai on my side of the car blasted a
phrase of Spanish at me that almost blew my hair
back. His face returned to stone and his gun remained pointed at my head. So this is what it's like
to "stare down the barrel of a gun." He must be
king of the mountain, I thought. Better not piss
him off.

"Um. Tu hablas Engles?" I squeaked.

The Moais surrounding the car broke into
simultaneous conversation while keeping one eye
on us as we sat rigidly in the car, smiles plastered
on our pale faces. Was this some sort of trick per-
petrated by the evil CIA? Were we spies or sabo-
teurs? Could we really be that stupid? A few guns
sagged to less threatening heights.

A man emerged from the building to our
right as schoolchildren marched up along the side-
walk and passed through the gate. They stepped in
front of him as if he didn't exist. There is something a bit surreal about six year-olds with, colorful
little school bags, chattering and skipping through
a forest of living Moais with guns. Especially while
we, two average white women sitting in a patheti-

cally little car, were gawked at like a traffic accident.

This was the man in charge. A cigarette dangled from his mouth and sleep creased his face. Sergeant Cigarette eyed us and barked. Stances firmed, guns raised, conversations stopped. King Moai approached Sergeant Cigarette. Through the barrier of humans surrounding our car, I could see them discussing the situation.

King Moai strode back to the car. He leaned down toward me. "Passports," he growled.

"Holy crap," I said. We fished for our passports — items we cherished more than our skis — knowing that the forfeiture of our only forms of identification could land us in a "serious situation." "Raped and dead," was another phrase that came to my mind. I considered my battered lifeless body carelessly tossed in a heap at the base of some trees left to openly rot. Back in the States, my mom would cry and demand information on my whereabouts from some government paper pusher who had neither an idea or care about my well-being. This collection of thoughts took only as long to pass through my mind as the amount of time it took me to dig out my passport. I felt a bit sick and yet irritated with myself for being such an idiot with foreign languages and perhaps driving directions.

We reluctantly handed them over. King Moai collected our passports and carried them over to Sergeant Cigarette who immediately disappeared back into the building, probably to sleep on it for a while.

Back to being the boss, King Moai decided to start the interrogation: "blah bitty blah bitty blah?" he barked. KO and I discussed our interpretations of his question. I tried to explain: "Nosotros es de Norte America. En vacacion aqui." Confused by my destruction of his native tongue, King Moai barked to a subordinate whose gun now hung by his side, cigarette in hand. He looked practically human. Leaning down to my window Private Benjamin said, "Where you come from?"

We were elated! Someone spoke English. We could get this all cleared up now and get on our way. Nervousness gave way to relief as we tumbled out an explanation. "We're from Chicago," we said. "Do you know Chicago?" I silently said, "bang-bang" the phrase for which our city has been known since the Al Capone era and the most common greeting by people with limited vocabulary. Chicago-Bang-Bang: The international name for our hometown. Perhaps we'd skip Chicago-Bang-Bang this time around.

"Oprah... Michael Jordan... Chicago Bulls..." I offered but received only a blank look

77

in return. "Don't these people have TVs?" I wondered. "Santiago," I then said and a small light registered.

"Why you come here?"

KO leaned over to explain. "We're here to go hiking in the mountains," she volunteered. "Hiking. Walking," she walked her fingers across her hand and smiled up at him.

"Why?" Private Benjamin persisted. His English skills were perhaps a bit more limited than we had hoped.

"To explore the mountain…. You know, to look at the trees and the flowers…" KO continued.

"Why?"

It slowly dawned on us that perhaps a leisure hike in the mountains is not considered fun or relaxing when you spend your life living at high altitudes. How does one explain the lure of the fresh air and solitude to someone who doesn't live amidst smog or crowded places? And further, to one who has a powerful gun designed to keep people like us out of places like that?

KO stuck with her explanation. She took the map from me and tried to show him the winding road ending in dot-dot-dot.

Our repeated attempts to explain seemed to only make us more guilty looking, like a cheating husband who comes home with a lengthy cho-

reographed response to his wife's simple: "hmmm, you're home late tonight." We decided to shut up.

Private Benjamin's gun accidentally banged against my car door as he turned to King Moai who stood smoking and watching us. Oh, that's gonna cost me, I automatically thought before returning to my litany of laments: turning over my passport, not telling anyone where we were going, drinking too much water. It would be insane to leave the security of our "Pop" car but Mother Nature was now pressing heavily on my kidneys.

About a hundred years passed. The mountain Moai returned to being humans, smoking in clusters chatting and mostly ignoring us. Just when I was feeling desperate enough to risk rape and murder for 30 seconds on a toilet Sergeant Cigarette re-emerged. Spanish was flying about us again, and Private Benjamin returned to my side. "Why two colors?" He meant that KO's passport was blue while mine was forest green, though both were U.S. documents.

I admitted that I didn't know, palms up, shrugging my shoulders and smiling.

"Get out of the car." Uh-oh. King Moai was back.

We reluctantly tore ourselves from the security of the "Pop" car, feeling exposed and uncertain again.

"Come."

We followed the King and Private Benjamin, not to the building on the right where Sergeant Cigarette was standing, but rather to a *Hogan's Heroes* kind of guardhouse on the left side of the road. "I know nuth-ink!" the line from *Hogan's Heroes*, came involuntarily into my head.

Crowded into the hut, we stood facing a window grimy from smoke and grit that looked down the road we had just come up. "Freedom," I inwardly sighed. On the desk lay a huge book the size of *Mother Goose and Grimm's Fairy Tales*. The rest of the desk and hut stood bare, the paint on the walls peeling and greasy from hundreds of guards over the years. The book's faded black cover was smeared and stained. Private Benjamin used both hands to heave it open.

"You sign now," they instructed us before giving back our passports. I took the pen and looked down, staring at a blank page in a huge book of a hundred blank pages. Clearly this little outpost of military life didn't get too many visitors. Realizing that we were likely to survive without any bodily harm, I giddily entered my information. I resisted signing it, "Love and Kisses, Lisa" before handing over the pen to KO who dutifully entered her information. She didn't seem to feel as excited about putting her name down in their book as I was.

The work done, we were escorted back to our car. In the snuggly protective comfort of the Pop-mobile we dutifully put on our seatbelts and prepared to leave. "OK well then," I said, "buh-bye!" and waved to the smoking circle. "It's been fun guys. Thanks for the hospitality!" I was on a roll.

Sergeant Cigarette leaned down to my window, unsmiling. Our faces were so close that the creases in his skin blurred. He exhaled ashtray at me, "You go back to Santiago *now!*"

"Yes, sir" I responded, swallowing my giddiness. I started the car without waiting for any further instructions or invitations.

My three-point turn to get out from there was more like a six-point turn, the road too narrow and the hut in my way. All that back and forth and back and forth allowed my personality to come back to center. It occurred to me that no one would ever believe this story. I'd need some proof. "Quick, KO," I said, "the camera."

She dove into the back and grabbed a disposable box camera out of her bag. We had only seconds as I had finally gotten the car pointing back down the mountain road toward freedom. I started to accelerate as her head popped up and she snapped a few quick photos of the mountain Moai, guns down watching us pull away.

"Got it!" she said and I pedaled as fast as I could to get our Fred Flintstone mobile out of there before they could react.

The Pop car back in motion beneath us felt good…in fact, *everything* felt good. We survived an encounter with the mountain Moai and had photos to prove it.

We immediately drove to the coast, ignoring King Moai's instructions to go to Santiago, and spent the night in a little town where we arose to the discovery of café con leche. More than just coffee with milk, it is a little sip of heaven. You get all your day's fat, sugar, and caffeine in one cup before the sun is fully up. After a well-earned night's sleep and a couple of delicious coffees, we had nearly forgotten the whole "gun-in-the-face-pee-in-your-pants" high altitude episode. There was still so much to see and do!

*   *   *

The trip ended too quickly and we were suddenly back in the chaos of the airport. Having over-shopped, we were forced to check some luggage for the flight home. KO volunteered her small navy blue cotton duffle. It held some clothes, our well-worn map, our Spanish-English dictionary, a disposable camera, and some other miscellaneous junk that we wouldn't need on the flight.

In Chicago we sailed through Immigration and stood shoulder-to-shoulder with the mob, snatching at luggage on the conveyor belt. KO spotted her navy duffle and grabbed it by one handle, revealing a "tear" at the seam. Upon inspection, we noticed someone had neatly sliced her duffle along the piping, leaving an almost invisible gap. We zipped it open and pulled out the contents, at first confused about what was missing. Then we realized that the disposable camera – the one containing the only photos of our adventure with the mountain Moais—had been removed.

There was no longer any evidence that the place existed.

ALIEN PLATEAU

I already didn't like him. We had only arrived in Lima a day earlier on a private expedition to seek out a "secret" cave in the Peruvian Andes, but I had taken an immediate disliking to our host. *Princess* Philip, as he was known in my mind only, was an adult English trust fund baby who lived on an "allowance" of about $10,000 per month, blowing the full amount and more on businesses and "girlfriends." In his home office the front of his desk was lined with eleven business card holders, each identifying him as president of yet another half-baked entity. And through his bedroom flowed a stream of "girlfriends" who, in exchange for an undisclosed amount of *soles*, would ensure that the Princess kept his creative business juices flowing.

"Ugh!" was all I could say to my client, Gil. "That man is a pig and he has no respect for women."

"Yeah," he agreed, but then dismissed Philip's childish and eccentric behavior. After all, he let us stay at his house and use his jeep (he had gotten a special stipend from his father for that month so that he could buy a new jeep, using our expedition as his excuse). Besides, from all that the Princess had told Gil, he was a local hero up in San Pedro, the town where we'd leave the vehicle and set out with our mule train of gear. It seems that he decided to improve the economy of this tiny high altitude village by having a large oven trucked up there so that they could have a bakery. With a bakery the villagers could make more bread and pizzas for the tourists. Pizzas for tourists seemed to be the big selling point in Philip's mind. It didn't bother him that the locals never asked for his bakery, that he never established a work schedule or hired employees, that they don't eat pizza, or that only about 100 non-Peruvian pizza eaters visited the village each year.

The mayor came out for the ribbon-cutting ceremony. He and Princess Philip shook hands. The mayor was very grateful; he had his photo taken several times. Princess Philip got in his car and drove back to Lima with his girlfriend du jour, satisfied that he had done something very generous. He was happy. He was going to have sex to celebrate. The mayor was also very happy. He thought about how much money he could make if he sold the equipment.

They say you never really know a person until you have traveled with them. That's when the idiosyncrasies and intolerances surface and the core of their personality emerges, exposing one's less-than-perfect side. In my years of leading trips around the globe, often to physically challenging or difficult locations, I occasionally see people turn ugly, subjecting their fellow travelers to tantrums, breakdowns, and outright nastiness. At the moment I was feeling no love for the Princess and had to keep myself in check. This was not about me; I was here for my client.

Gil is a truly unique individual: intelligent, well connected and wealthy; on the surface he's a great catch. For those who have never met him, they expect I should be attracted to him. However, my first rule of business is never to "mix" with the clients. Besides, neither of us felt the slightest emotion for the other. I appreciated that he never hit on me, which allowed us to take these odd adventures without worries of awkward sexual tension. We'd catch up on each other's lives as we hiked up dusty trails, analyzing behaviors or sharing stories of loves gone awry. Gil had a greater degree of patience for the Princess and looked at his stream of paid girlfriends as a way for him to improve the economic situations of these women. They did come voluntarily, after all.

I didn't share his patience and bristled at the lack of respect the Princess showed all women, not just his "girlfriends." When we met, Philip explained that he had moved to Lima almost thirty years earlier because "it's cheap, and the women are some of the most beautiful in the world." I was impressed by his compliments towards the women of Peru until he added: "and all my girlfriends are very cheap." I made the mistake of wondering aloud if they were really girlfriends since they only showed up when *he* wanted sex and *they* needed money. He's hated me ever since.

After several hours winding up a harrowing steep and occasionally one-lane ribbon of a road that caresses the edge of the range, we arrived at the arid village of San Pedro, gateway to Marcahuasi (pronounced Mark-a-whaa-see). I was brought on board to be the ropes expert for a vertical descent into the cave, but during preparations I was more interested in the physical characteristics of our destination. I was only now learning about the Marcahuasi Plateau and it's spiritual significance.

Gil and Philip explained to me how Marcahuasi had been discovered in the 1950s by a man named Dr. Daniel Ruzo. I never learned what he earned his doctorate in or if indeed he really had a degree at all. He was, though, a "leading expert" on the plateau. This translation of the introduction to his book published in the 1970s set the scene about which I was to enter:

"Our discoveries were made like this: observing rocks near where thousands of people lived, but they didn't see them because they lacked faith in the magic world and in the works of art left by a former humanity which created and respected this world and produced these incomparable works of art, but left no signature. The artistic work was the rhythm of life, like heartbeats, or breathing, or walking on this earth. It was a work of magic. Humanity has forgotten all of this and considers going to the moon much more important. It cannot explain the appearance of these genius men who break all barriers to arrive at surprising results without seeking for himself, and without listening to dogmatic voices—which try to reduce to words that which has no name.

We demonstrate in this book that the carvings and the sculptures made in the natural rock, to be seen from a point of view or a certain direction, and in conditions of special lighting, give credit to a style that could only be expressed by men of profound pantheist faith. The technique of these sculptors has not been repeated in subsequent history. These works are found in different places on earth, very removed from one another, repeating the same symbols, and with one thing in common:

they are found around sacred mountains, temples of lost humanity, so they won't be forgotten and that they may serve one more time to purify and save humanity."

Hmmmm. So let me get this straight... I ticked off the major points:

1.   This plateau is covered with rocks that were carved by a "former" race of humans.

2.   No remnants of this race of humans exist except the "carved" stones.

3.   The tools of these craftsmen or artists have never been discovered.

4.   The resulting art can only be seen from certain vantage points or when the sun is at a particular angle in the sky.

5.   Oh, and they are best viewed by people who have faith in the magic world.

Philip enthusiastically told me about the art I should expect to see on the cave walls left by aliens who had visited the plateau. He was certain we would find this art because he was an "expert" on aliens. After all, he used to have a radio program at 5am on Sundays where he would discuss visitations by aliens or UFO sightings... that was, until it was cancelled. They had also cancelled his all-1970s rock show on which he was known as "Philip The Beat." Oh, my God! I didn't even *ask* about body probing. He was probably an expert on that, too.

What had I gotten myself into??

When Gil asked me to work with him on this expedition, he had told me what he knew from his previous dozen trips to the plateau. A long time ago, he said, when he first came to the plateau he had been told a story by his guide, Don Manuel, that had been niggling at his curiosity ever since. Don Manuel worked as an assistant to Dr. Ruzo back in the 1950s when he was studying the plateau. One day, they discovered this cave and Dr. Ruzo lowered Don Manuel down into the cave to explore. He never had a chance to explore it though because he became "very hot" and frightened. He insisted that he be pulled up. Their belief that this secret cave was an access point to part of the 'mystical world' kept anyone from ever trying to re-enter it. Over the years it had apparently been forgotten by everyone but Don Manuel, who was an old man by now.

Gil wanted to be the first to explore the cave, and I was happy to be a part of the team. After all, I was curious too. Unless this area was volcanic, how could it be hot down in a cave above 12,000 feet? And why didn't anyone else ever try to explore it? Where was it in relation to anything else on the plateau? What was this plateau like? I couldn't wait to get there.

The Princess and Girlfriend du Jour headed up on horseback leaving the distribution of equipment and packing of the mules to Gil and me. Fortunately, the locals were elated to have an opportunity to rent out their animals to these loco rich guys so we had the town square filled with helpers and observers alike. I spent time taking photos of the women in their black stovepipe hats and brightly woven ponchos while Gil distributed photos he had taken on a previous visit. Always generous from the heart, Gil didn't just snap and then hand out Polaroids, he returned home with rolls of film that he would develop, crop, enlarge, and color adjust. Returning on his next visit he'd give away 8" x 10" photos to these remote locals who likely would never see a picture of themselves. The joy of receiving the photos was evident.

Before we left town, Gil and I visited the town's museum, a wooden building with a solid layer of dust on the display cases. In this single room, I saw the true story of the plateau emerge: "mummies" of brown bones with their knees hugged to their chests had been extracted from vertical circular graves somewhere up on the plateau. Now *this* was interesting! An actual civilization apparently lived on the plateau several hundreds of years ago. Why weren't they investigating *that?*

Ah, but Gil explained to me, the mystical human race that carved the stones on the plateau

came thousands and thousands of years before these mummies, which was much more interesting.

"So you believe the alien stuff?"

Well, he admitted, he wasn't sure. He did say he was living proof that UFOs exist. He saw one hover above him up on the plateau on his first visit to the cave. That explained why he kept going back… he wanted to see another one.

Now if I could be up there when a UFO visited, that would be *really* interesting! However…

The use of hallucinogenic plants in shamanistic ceremonies is common practice in Peru. In this region the brew is called "san pedro," like the town, and is made from a particular type of cactus found in the mountains. People from all over the world come to have "experiences" while under the influence of hallucinogens in sacred ceremonies led by local shamans. I can't judge the people or practice because I've never done it myself. I do wonder though why UFOs only seem to appear when one is "under the influence" so to speak. I must have raised my eyebrow.

No! Gil assured me he was stone cold sober when the UFO appeared.

Hmmmm, this was getting interesting.

By the time we arrived on the plateau, a bit out of breath from the high altitude, we found the

Princess ordering the shaman around like a common hired hand. Apparently his disrespect knows no bounds. The Princess needed someone to inflate the mattress in his 3-room tent, load in and unpack his luggage bags, and start preparing the coca tea.

Wait a minute, back up: an inflatable queen-size mattress and a 3-room tent?! This guy was such an idiot. He had been complaining that Gil and I had taken too much stuff and wanted us to leave some technical equipment behind so that he could bring up his "basic supplies." Now that I saw the mound of "basic supplies" I felt even less love for the selfish Princess as I unpacked my single bag and one-person tent. Ugh! I reminded myself to be nice.

Don Manuel's sons joined us, all grown men eager to take part in the discovery of their father's secret cave. As the sun set and the temperature dropped like a stone into the mid-forties, we circled together and shivered our way through a ceremony to bless the cave site and workers, and to bless Gil for coming and making this discovery a reality.

As we gathered I noticed Girlfriend du Jour was turning blue in her light sweater and heels. Originally from Iquitos, the hot and humid city along the Amazon River in the north of Peru, she had no idea that it got cold up in the mountains.

The Princess didn't seem inclined to offer her any-thing so I gave her one of my fleeces and shivered a bit myself. Better that two people are a little cold than one totally frozen.

Was this a night for san pedro? I hoped to have a chance to watch people go through the ceremony, more so out of a desire witness the hallucinations than actually have any of my own, though I didn't discount the possibility of partak-ing. After all, one cannot criticize something they really no nothing about. The shaman chanted and we smoked all natural cigarettes. The proper tech-nique was to not actually inhale but rather suck the smoke into your mouth like a cigar and then blow it toward the cave. The shaman kept chanting and I kept shivering. A dome of stars grew brighter overhead in the crystal night air. When he was through we broke up and headed for dinner; ap-parently there would be no hallucinating tonight. Darn.

Our meal was light and mostly vegetables, and we partook of some whiskey that Gil had picked up down in the village. Good thinking, Gil. We stood around our small fire trying to keep warm chatting and planning for the start of our work on the cave in the morning. Suddenly the Princess cried out: "Look! A UFO!" and pointed toward a bright light in the sky.

"Philip," I said, "that's Venus."

"How do you know?" he challenged.

"Ok," I said, "I'll admit I'm not an astronomer but I'm almost positive that's Venus."

The Princess ignored me.

"Look!" he cried again a few moments later, excitedly pointing toward a light in the sky that was clearly moving and seemed much closer to us than the rest of the heavens.

"Philip," I shook my head in disbelief. "That's a plane."

It doesn't take a scientific leap to realize that the Lima International Airport is relatively close and the international flights were taking off into the night. I wasn't trying to burst his bubble. I would have been happy to see a UFO if a real UFO appeared, but this business of trying to make ordinary things into UFOs just to say that you've seen one seemed a bit childish.

The rest of the crowd shuffled uncomfortably and in a few moments I found myself standing alone. They all faced the same direction, (towards Venus and the plane) eager to spot UFOs without the annoying intrusion of reality coming from me with every "sighting." At the moment they were staring hard directly at the horizon where a light appeared to be "dancing about."

"Ah-ha!"

Oh, I knew what was coming next.

"A UFO! It's right there on the horizon.

See it? It's standing still right now. Oh! It just zoomed left. Now right... right... up... down... left... up... right...left... left..."

The play-by-play was killing me but I bit my lip. I could see a star on the horizon, and yes it appeared to be moving. Now, if I were a young child, innocent of deep scientific knowledge you gain by occasionally staying awake in high school science class, I might indeed think this was a UFO. But since both of the English-speaking grown men standing before me had at least high school diplomas I could only think that they either forgot or dismissed a few bits of known, proven, basic science.

"You guys," I interrupted the gleeful UFO spotters, "that's a star. Because you are looking at it directly across the horizon, the effects of the atmosphere make the star appear to move. Just watch it arc higher into the sky. You'll see that it stops dancing as it rises off the horizon."

"Why can't you just believe?" the Princess snapped.

"I would love to see a UFO. Really, I would. But I can't just suspend my knowledge because I want something to be something that it's not."

"How do you know that it's not a UFO?" the Princess pouted.

"Why can't you believe we're right?" Gil asked.

I recalled as best I could what my science teachers had tried to drill into our unformed minds and then tried again to explain how air in the atmosphere moves, causing light to be refracted in different directions, and how it is most noticeable along the horizon. It is not that the object itself is moving, but rather the light that is coming from it appeared to be moving.

There was stony silence.

"You just don't want to believe that UFOs really exist."

"No, it's not that." I could see that this was a matter of belief. The people on that side were not inclined to believe that there was a scientific explanation for the movement of light in the sky any more than I was inclined to suspend my belief in science and accept that alien spaceships were darting around undetected and so close to earth.

It was a draw. Girlfriend du Jour and the shaman had remained noticeably quiet throughout. She probably didn't know enough English to understand what was going on, but the shaman quite possibly really didn't know that it could be explained by science. And let's face it, it'd be bad for business if the rich Americans and Brits and Europeans stopped hiring him to join them on the plateau in search of UFO because they no longer believed that's what they were seeing.

Between the chilly air and the cold shoulders I sensed it was time for me to head to bed. I said goodnight and walked off into the dark. Tucked into my cozy sleeping bag, I made some notes and read for a bit, then turned off my light. There was quite a bit of commotion outside for a minute and then Gil appeared outside my tent. "Lisa!" he exclaimed, "You just missed one that flew really close to the plateau!"

Yeah, right, I thought. Now that I've gone to bed and the likelihood that I'll come back out is pretty slim, ET shows up.

"Darn," I said. "Maybe it'll come back tomorrow when I'm still out there. Good night."

Whoever said: "seeing is believing" never met a bunch of avid UFO enthusiasts. I think their motto is: *Believing is Seeing.*

I AM SURVIVED

Moises raised his machete. With a fast short chop he whacked the back leg of a large bullfrog—that had the misfortune of crossing into our camp—and then walked away. My thoughts went from "Breakfast!" to "What the...?" as I watched the bullfrog attempt to escape. With its lame leg it didn't make much progress.

We began our second day without food and I was getting a bit hungry. I also had cramps and was bleeding. This was not the stuff of *guy adventure stories* ; you know, the ones where they tie a tourniquet with their teeth around the stump of a severed limb or dragging their broken body over a thousand miles of pointy rocks in a place so un-inhabited that God doesn't even visit—or the ones where they wrestle six alligators as piranhas nip at their feet. I was not severed, broken, or nipped. I was giving birth to an alien trying to kick its way out of my abdomen by pushing off my spine. I was experiencing the full-on, monthly "joy of womanhood." Yeah, whatever.

The frog hopped in a wide circle and then I realized that we were not to have it as a meal...not just yet. My heart sank, my stomach growled and my alien kicked.

Four clients had joined me for a three-day jungle survival on a remote tributary in the Peruvian Amazon basin. When we set out yesterday morning we were clean and excited as we loaded our skimpy packs into the small boat that would transport us to the edge of the Tamshiyacu Reserve. For the next three days we would build our own shelter and live off the land either catching or killing all our food. We were allowed to bring only the shirt on our back, a poncho (in case we ran into a wasp nest), sleeping sheet, water bottle and purifier, mosquito net and repellent. I also packed my "necessities" as there are some rules that go unspoken.

Ten minutes down the river on Day One and we were already dripping with sweat. My stomach growled. Our guide Moises points out the "jungle candy" tree as we motor along the river deeper and deeper up a tributary. Unhurried, we stop and pick a few. The "fruit" is inside long, flat, dark green bean pods that overhang the river. Once you pry the pod open you pop the hard bean into your mouth to savor the sweet fuzzy coating. Mostly, it gives your mouth something to do, and soon I tire of the effort required to roll the inedible bean around in my cheeks without getting it lodged it in my throat.

I spit the last of my jungle candy into the river as we stop to photograph a morpho butterfly sunning itself on a branch along the bank. With large iridescent blue wing tops, it is a prized addition to any butterfly collection. When a morpho senses danger though, it closes its wings exposing the profile of a large snakehead with a big black circle of an eye. It's a terrific bit of genetically engineered self-preservation, as most birds won't swoop in on a snake. We take turns trying to snap photos of the palm-sized, snake-faced wings while not rocking the boat or scaring it off.

Patiently waiting, Moises glances into the trees ninety degrees to the right and sees a poisonous red tree snake also sunning itself on some branches above the water. He leans over towards me and softly asks, "Do you want to eat it?"

"Yes!" I whisper enthusiastically. I had learned food was not as plentiful as one might expect in such a green place, and that after a few days of not catching or killing anything else, we would likely partake of "grubby bugs," the fat white larvae found in the trunks of rotting trees. Mmmmm. I was all for a dinner of snake.

Moises reaches into the bottom of the boat and picks up an old spear with a metal triton head. Without ceremony he launches it at the snake. The prongs of the triton hit its mark, piercing the snake through the body just past its head, pinning it to the tree branch. I am stunned. Had I been the one to throw the spear, it would surely now be sinking to the bottom of the river, while the unscathed snake would go on living another day.

I was elated and the others surprised at what transpired in the time it took them to snap a few photos. We immediately forgot the morpho. "Dinner!" It looked like we wouldn't have to eat grubby bugs after all.

We happily continue up the river stopping again, this time to hike through someone's farm. Banish all notions of a farm that you would find in America's breadbasket. Each year the Amazon spills up to forty miles beyond its banks during the rainy season. Anyone living within those forty miles has a house on stilts, no electricity, and land that will spend several months under water. Farms in the Amazon Basin are simple plots of reasonably cleared jungle that may be home to a cow, some pigs, a few chickens, or perhaps banana and papaya trees. Root vegetables or ground runners such as squash could never survive the wet soil, and farmers must be vigilant to protect the few other crops they may plant, as the jungle is filled with many hungry creatures that consider a farm to be more like a large salad bar.

The farmer was ankle deep in muck, making a lackadaisical effort to clear the forever-encroaching growth away. No one moves quickly in these parts, especially in the oppressive humidity of the rainy season. But we weren't there to admire his muddy clearing; we sought the barbasco trees in the jungle beyond his farm where we would dig out and hack off some of their roots for reasons that still weren't clear to me.

The barbasco tree root has a unique property that always makes me wonder what drove a person to discover its use. Now, on Day Two of our survival, our guides told us we'd learn what exactly this unique property was. We were going fishing.

We clambered into the boat and motored further up the tributary. Today, the river was seven feet higher as it had rained a solid twelve hours through the night. I was beginning to appreciate what the "rainy season" meant here in the Amazon Basin.

Our guides had helped us build our shelter during the afternoon of Day One after we climbed up the bank of the river at a place they thought suitable. Our wall-less shelter was a simple construction, roughly twelve feet long and six feet wide supported by the trunks of six young trees we had cut from the edge of the rainforest. Our roof consisted of woven mats of long palm fronds lain across the slender trunks of several more trees we had cut down. The "floor" was also covered in unwoven palm fronds cut from other trees, on which we laid our sleeping sheets. Directly above our sleeping sheets we each hung our mosquito nets from vines tied to the felled trees that now served as cross beams for our roof. We had spent hours chopping, dragging, pounding, weaving, laying, and tying this masterpiece of green and brown. And then the rain had begun.

Windless, the rain fell in a solid mass that turned the air white. There were no waves of heavier or lighter rain. It was like sleeping under the cascade of a waterfall for twelve hours—sunset to sunrise almost exactly. The Peruvians call this deluge "Man's Rain."

Moises and his assistant Josias refused our help building their shelter, and when the rain started, we were happy enough to get under our palm frond canopy and marvel at the degree of dryness our handiwork provided. I detected only a single drip…directly above my head. Despite the early hour of sunset in the Amazon, we quickly fell asleep to the music of rain in the jungle.

Moises and Josias never finished their shelter and so they spent the night in the boat under a tarp, ineffectively bailing out the ever-accumulating rain with a flat-faced paddle. Throughout the night what we thought was muffled thunder was actually the wooden paddle as it hit the metal sides of the boat. In the morning Moises and Josias were tired and unhappy. I now realized why they had tried to load tents into the boat.

Before departing from the lodge, as students eager for the full survival experience, we had insisted the tents remain on the dock. "Ha," we sneered, "We don't need no steek-in' tents." Moises gave in with a shrug. "I am survived," he said in his laconic manner, and turned away disappointed.

The morning of Day Two was a disappointment for us as well. Having not eaten for a day, we looked forward to dining on the poisonous red tree snake that we hadn't had time to cook before the rain started. With the approach of dawn, however, I learned a dear lesson about survival in the Amazon: dead things don't last in the heat and humidity of the jungle. The huge amount of bacteria in the Amazon begins the decaying process almost immediately. Our uncooked snake had begun to decompose.

Without ceremony Moises took the snake and dumped it in the river. "Augh!" I cried, "That was breakfast!"

With my stomach growling as our boat pulled away destined for the fishing grounds, where we would use the mysterious barbasco roots that were piled at my feet, I now understood why the frog was still alive. By cutting it's tendon it would not be able to hop away, and by leaving it alive it would still be fresh for us to eat tonight for dinner. Moises wasn't being cruel. He was being smart. The thought of frog for dinner made me salivate.

Fishing in the Amazon with barbasco roots during the rainy season is a bit trickier than one would expect. First, you must hike for about a week (with cramps and without food) through the steaming jungle in search of a slow-moving section of river. After 12 solid hours of rain, there is no such thing as a river that is not moving fast no matter how long you walk. This means you must hack up more small trees to throw in the river to create a dam pathetic enough to allow the water and fish to pass through but sturdy enough to slow down the current. The fish will then gather along the banks of the "slow zone."

In the meantime, because our only tools were a machete and spear, we had to pound the barbasco roots into a pulp with a makeshift club chopped from a thick branch. Crouching like a native while beating on the roots against the base of a huge tree was uncomfortable for the others, but it made my cramps less painful, so I hogged the homemade club leaving my fellow survivors to search for skinny trees and vines. There was still more clear-cutting to be done in the name of survival.

With each of our tasks completed, we used the vines to tie pulped roots to one end of fist-thick trees then dunked them into the slow zone creating milky-white clouds in the water. Our water still moved too quickly so our clouds appeared like artistic swirls, tie-dying the chocolate river as they bled downstream.

We now discovered the barbasco's unique quality: it paralyzes a fish's gills forcing it to come to the surface to breathe. Once they come to the surface, we were able to spear them. Now again I ask, who thought it a good idea to hike into the jungle to dig up some tree roots so that they could smash them up and dunk them in a river in the hope that it would make fish surface? My tribe would have been weaving nets of vines.

The stunned fish coming into our liquid lair were few and far between. They were also undersized and emaciated. And yet we hunted them with enthusiasm and celebrated the spearing of each scrawny one. Two hours later we had caught only a small pail, each of us having speared at least one, when Moises decided we were done.

Someone once said, "We are only five meals away from being barbarians." Our tiny band of survival students had gone without four meals already, and we looked hungrily into the pail mentally dividing up the loot. "Jungle sushi!" I volunteered, ready to eat them raw. Moises protectively took the pail. Apparently, to a man willing to dine on live squiggling larva fished from the belly of decaying tree trunks, uncooked fish was an inedible concept.

We set out on the hike back to the boat, catching up with Josias who had been busy chopping down a 30' tree for reasons we didn't understand until he showed us a foot-long section of white wood that came from near the top. Ah, so that's what heart of palm looks like when it's not in a can! Inwardly I cringed at the thought of a 30' tree being cut down for a little section of edible insides and made a mental note to stop buying hearts of palm. Josias offered us a sample from an end as thick as my wrist, and even though I was starving and making a mental picture of dining on a salad at home tossed with coin-size cuts of heart of palm in a light balsamic vinegar dressing at a table surrounded by friends and wine and more food to come, it tasted like chewable wood. Apparently, the stuff that comes in a can is farmed, cut very young, and still tender. Mental note to self: go ahead and buy the canned stuff.

Finally, back at camp and after quite a bit of effort, we got a fire going and put the bucket on to boil. Tonight's Menu: fish stew with roasted frog. Oh my god. I was in heaven! We were going to eat something that was cooked—real live meat, of sorts anyway.

Moises extracted a plastic baggie of what looked like pieces of broken teeth yellowed from smoking and explained that this was tapioca, the only staple he allowed brought from civilization. His words brought visions of tapioca pudding from my childhood—that sweet, creamy dessert treat that mom would occasionally dole out if we finished our dinner. But the sight of Moises's plastic bag made my teeth hurt.

I don't know if it's a Peruvian custom, survival technique, cruel joke, or just lack of cooking knowledge, but Moises never put the stuff in water. When the thin fish stew was ready, he gave us each a small handful of the tapioca to grind between our teeth. We masticated the rocky flavorless chunks into sizes that could be swallowed. I tried to soak my handful in the half-cup of warm fish-flavored Amazon River water I had been allocated, but it did nothing to soften the tapioca and my hunger was too great to care. I ate the broken tooth gravel hoping my own teeth would survive.

My short dining experience was only interrupted by a needle-sized bone from an undernourished fish that simultaneously pierced the roof of my mouth and tongue locking my mouth in a startled "O." I still didn't care. I reached in and plucked it out making sure there was no meat on it before I tossed it into the jungle behind me and went back to my meal.

Over the fire hovered our frog, skinless and skewered. It smelled delicious. Once out of his skin he looked much smaller than the Clincher softball he started out as, and I obsessed that he might fall into the pile of hot ash. The faces of my companions mirrored my concern as we all stared attentively to ensure our frog remained above the flames. When pulled from the heat and split amongst seven people, I sat looking at my portion—roughly a tablespoon of thigh meat. I nibbled at it, savoring the single bite as long as I could. And then dinner was abruptly over.

Like vultures, we had left the fish and frog carcasses spotless; which required very little in the area of general clean up. After flinging the skeletons into the swiftly moving water, we sat around our dimming fire and watched the sun "set"—an impossible task when surrounded by 50 foot-tall trees. I slipped away to take care of my "girl business" and returned with no less than a thousand mosquito bites on my thighs and bum. I have no idea how the native women handle this every month here in a place where mosquitoes look at humans and see a sign that says "Over A Billion

Served." Guys really don't know how good they have it.

After the wetness of the night before, you'd think we'd welcome dusk without rain, but it brought a fresh hatch of mosquitoes that swarmed our little party, clouding the air around us. Flailing at the thirsty demons, we dashed to our shelter and dove under our mosquito nets. In the dark I grabbed my headlamp and turned it on.

Strung from above, each mosquito net drops down like a gossamer coffin, leaving enough to tuck under your body if only part way. Now, sitting inside my mosquito net coffin, my headlamp on, I sat face-to-face with a poisonous white palm spider the size of a pie plate. "Help..." I squeaked.

No reply.

"You guys, help. Please." I was rooted to the spot, afraid to move an inch for fear I'd startle my visitor causing it to leap onto my face and bite me between the eyes, injecting a deadly amount of venom almost directly into my brain. By the time they'd get me back to civilization, my head would be swollen to the size of a basketball and, as I'd learned from our snake, I'd have partially decomposed. No, I wasn't going anywhere.

"What's the matter?" Kathy asked. She lay immediately to my left. "Holy....." She saw the spider's shadow cast on her mosquito net.

"There's a really, really big spider in here," I said, keeping my voice soft as if not to disturb it.

"Don't look at me," Ren said without rolling over. "I'm scared to death of spiders."

"Me, too," Kathy added, staring at the large shadow.

To my right Scott remained silent, feigning sleep. That left Andy to my far left. "Please, Andy, help..." Heroically, he emerged from the protection of his mosquito net and strode past the others until he was outside my coffin.

"Holy shit," he said. "That thing is huge!"

"I know."

Scott gave up his pretend sleep now that Andy had stepped back out into the cloud of mosquitoes. He slid his broad rimmed hat from under his net to Andy and looked over at the focus of all headlamps. "Christ, that thing is huge!"

Andy carefully pulled my netting away from my face as he reached under and cupped Scott's hat around the spider. I shimmied back not wanting to be in the way in case my large visitor got free. Andy dragged the hat down the netting, shifting it to keep the big hairy legs all contained, and swooped the whole package into the black jungle.

I breathed for the first time in a long minute. My heart was pounding in my ears, and I shivered despite the heat and humidity. Scott could go retrieve his hat in the morning. Thanks for nothing, you big chicken, I thought. "Thanks, Andy," I said.

"No problem," he replied and returned to his net, swinging and swatting along the way. The silence felt a bit awkward as we all lay in the dark contemplating our own reactions. I don't fear much, but a poisonous spider as big as my face, *in* my face, had me a bit freaked out. My reaction was surprisingly girly, and perhaps there was a small desire for someone else to help me extricate it so that they too could appreciate its enormity. It's never a very good story if you're the only one who can tell it.

The night air resonated with the music and rustling of jungle creatures, snoring companions, and Kathy as she swatted and cursed at an unseen pest. I had my own problems tracking down the mosquitoes that had gotten in when the spider was let out, but soon exhaustion took over, and I slipped into unconsciousness, occasionally slapping at my diners with a groggy hand.

At the first hint of daylight, Kathy was up and practically in tears from lack of sleep and disgust. The unseen pests were now visible—by the thousands. As my eyes adjusted to thin morning light, I realized that I, too, was not alone.

In the night an endless stream of termites had exited the large old tree adjacent to where Kathy and I slept. Not deterred by the mosquito nets, they climbed up the support post of our shelter between our coffins and tracked along the vines that suspended our mosquito nets, entering where the two meet. The busy little buggers then hiked back down and past our heads, along the inside of our nets toward our feet. While Kathy, a light sleeper, spent the night awake and slapping termites off her skin, I drowsily rolled over a thick column of them as they crossed along the ground heading, apparently, for my boots. I now had a layer of squished termites running down the right side of my face and body. I was so dirty that I carelessly squeegeed them off my skin, bits remaining squished and stuck along the way. Having learned they make a great mosquito repellent, I rubbed the rest in like a lotion.

Termites are attracted to salt, and Kathy's daypack was their holy grail. In the morning light we could see hundreds of happy termites creating a new mound on the sweat-coated surface of her pack. "I've got spooge all over my pack!" she wailed.

The termites had also found great dining in our boots, and we all had to thump them on the ground to expel the hordes. This was also a great way to get rid of any snakes or other jungle creatures that decided to call your boots home in the night, and I diligently thumped to ensure my spider guest had not returned. The termites spared only Andy, probably more a result of distance than good karma for his spider eviction, but one never knows. He still gave his boots a solid smack on the ground, not wanting to push the good karma thing too far. Day Three was off to a good start.

Breakfast was a rumble in the stomach as we tromped back into the jungle to cut down yet another tree. It seemed like survival meant clear-cutting the rainforest, and the environmentalist in me cringed with each whack from the machete. Today, we cut down a tree that would supply us with cacao. We were guaranteed that this would produce "a delicious drink like chocolate milk."

After wearing himself out, Andy passed the machete to Ren and stepped back. A moment later he was dancing and cussing, madly slapping at his legs. And then his pants came off.

Fire ants are cruel little things that you never feel climbing up your skin until they decide to take a bite out of you. By then it's too late. Andy had apparently stepped into a trail of ants that simply rerouted themselves up his pant legs. They had found a patch of skin on his calf that was already raw, and the lingering sting from their bites was unbearable. He cursed and danced and swatted at himself until he was free from the intruders and his clothing. So much for his good karma. With eyes constantly scanning the ground, we quickly finished our task, harvested the nuts from the top of the fallen tree, and headed back to camp.

Like a scene from *Planet of the Apes* , we bashed the nuts open with rocks, then ground up the insides and dropped them in our little fish pot. While Andy spun between his hands a small knobby branch to blend the "chocolate milk" cooking in the pot over the fire, we went down to the river to refill our water supply. Dash all thoughts of a blue river when you think of the Amazon and its tributaries. The Amazon comes in two colors: tea and cappuccino—a result of the mountainous volume of decay that occurs in the Amazon jungle. Swimming in the river is surreal (think: the opening scene from *Jaws*); you cannot see your body beneath the surface of the water, nor can you see the creatures below that might like to eat you. Very creepy.

On Day Two while our fish and frog dinner cooked, I had leapt into the river to save my camera from an unfortunate tumble into the water and was swept away by the swift current from the nightlong rainfall. I found myself quickly around a bend before I was able to grab onto some overhanging vines and stop my flush toward the mighty Amazon River. I decided that was enough "swimming" for me and pulled myself out. Scott, however, thought it looked like fun and threw himself in to take the same joy ride. "Woo!" he hollered in mid-air. "Ouch!" he yelled on impact. Scott

122

had hit a submerged tree branch and was flushed around the bend. He hastily exited the river, re-thinking his strategy for entertainment.

Now, as Kathy extracted the water purifier tube from the river as it bobbed under the edge of the boat, she pulled up a scorpion that had stopped to rest on the Styrofoam ball used to keep the tube from sinking to the gritty bottom. There seemed to be no end to the interactions with Amazon wild-life for us, except perhaps with the edible ones.

Apparently in the Amazon the words choc-olate and chalk are interchangeable. Though Andy had been churning away until his arms were weak, our brew remained grainy brown water desperately in need of sugar and flavor, neither of which we could expect to arrive any time soon. So we drank down the granular tree-flavored, lukewarm water hoping it held at least some nutritional value.

Another "meal" quickly consumed, it was time to head back into the jungle. Our lesson: learn how to weave backpacks from palm fronds, which of course, required us to kill off more trees.

By mid-afternoon we had exhausted the ba-sic survival skills that Moises and Josias could teach us, everyone a bit listless from hunger though still not hungry enough to start scratching grubby bugs out of rotting trees. We gathered our few belong-ings and piled into the boat for our journey home with only a short glance back at our jungle camp.

It was a good hour and a half down the river to our electricity-free, cold shower, lodge-on-stilts in the rainforest, but it felt like we were motoring towards heaven.

On the ride back I discovered that everyone else had snuck food along in their packs, though they all said it remained untouched. "Technically, we're done, so who wants to share Ren's bag of peanuts from the plane," I tempted them. They all refused to break down and give in to hunger now when they were so close to officially completing their 3-Day Survival Course. We instead hungrily grabbed jungle candy off trees as we passed them and found a lone passion fruit to share its sour, immature contents.

Upon arrival at our electricity-free lodge, we were greeted by the staff that did their best to not cringe or turn away from the smell radiating from our sweaty and dirty band of survival students. We emptied our meager supplies from the boat onto the dock next to the tents we had left three days earlier bundled up, clean, and ready to go.

"Hey!" Ren asked Moises, "Does this mean that now 'I am survived?'"

"Yes," Moises answered in his slow deep voice. "You are survived."

LISA GREYHILL

Lisa Greyhill co-founded Adventure Travelers Society in 1997. To date, she has visited over 50 countries, shaken hands with the presidents of Chile and Rwanda, and been robbed by Parisians, Ticos, and monkeys. She has jumped out of planes, skied over cliffs, body surfed at night in a sea of phytoplankton, swam with piranhas, sharks, and pink dolphins, been shoved by a silverback, spit on by camels and llamas, and bitten by a brown recluse spider. Lisa has also been dragged behind a car, smashed her face into pavements and windows, and cut off her finger. Only some of these things were intentional.

Lisa's goal is to ski or hike every major mountain range in the world.

CORNERSTONE PRESS

CEO: Dan Dieterich
President: Donna Collins
Corporate Secretary: Christine Mosnik
Editor-In-Chief: Peggy Farrell
Associate Editor-In-Chief: Andrew Ilk
Managing Editor: Ryan Ostopowicz
Associate Managing Editor: Trina Olson
Business Manager: Tara Cook
Production Manager: Sara Jensen
Designer: Joy Ratchman
Associate Designer: Colin McGinnis
Marketing Manager: Chuck Zoromski
Advertising Manager: Michael Philleo
Publicity Director: Amanda Fisher
Associate Publicity Director: Felicia Ciula
Associate Publicity Director: Chris Warren
Sales Manager: Dale Bratz, Jr.
Substance Editor: Maggie Hanson
Associate Substance Editor: Jennifer White
Copy Editor: Nelson Carvajal
Associate Copy Editor: Aimee Freston
Associate Copy Editor: Ingrid Nordstrom
Associate Copy Editor: David Stelter
Associate Copy Editor: Daniel Henke
Fulfillment Manager: Andrea Vesely
Webmaster: Jason Roskos